THE APPROACH TO THE
SOCIAL QUESTION

THE APPROACH TO THE SOCIAL QUESTION

AN INTRODUCTION TO THE STUDY OF
SOCIAL ETHICS

BY

FRANCIS GREENWOOD PEABODY

PLUMMER PROFESSOR OF CHRISTIAN MORALS IN
HARVARD UNIVERSITY

WIPF & STOCK · Eugene, Oregon

Wipf and Stock Publishers
199 W 8th Ave, Suite 3
Eugene, OR 97401

The Approach to the Social Question
An Introduction to the Study of Social Ethics
By Peabody, Francis Greenwood
ISBN 13: 978-1-5326-1088-2
Publication date 10/3/2016
Previously published by The Macmillan Company, 1909

TO A. T. W.

WHOM DOES THE MASTER CHOOSE TO BE HIS FRIEND?
WHOM DOES HE TRUST HIS WANDERING FLOCK TO TEND?
NOT HIM WHOSE CREED IS LONGEST, OR WHOSE PRAISE
ECHOES THE CERTITUDES OF OTHER DAYS;
BUT THE TRAINED LEADER IN THE WORLD'S FIERCE STRIFE,
WHOSE FAITH IS SERVICE AND WHOSE WORSHIP LIFE;
WHOSE LAVISH HEART SERVES WITH FAR-SEEING EYES,
WHOSE TRUTH IS MERCY, AND WHOSE PITY WISE;
TO WHOM POSSESSIONS MAKE AN OPEN DOOR
TO SAVE THE CITY AND TO SERVE THE POOR;
WHOSE MONUMENTS OF UNRECORDED GOOD
ESCAPE THE PRAISES OF THE MULTITUDE.
THE DWELLERS IN THE CITY'S WILDERNESS
FEEL THE STRONG TOUCH OF HIS FIRM GENTLENESS,
AND THEIR HEARTS OPEN TO THE MASTER-KEY
OF HIS ALL-COMPREHENDING CHARITY.
ACROSS THE AGES SPEAKS THE SON OF MAN:
"FOR SUCH GOD'S KINGDOM WAITS SINCE TIME BEGAN;
THIS, WHICH YE DO SO SELF-EFFACINGLY
UNTO THESE LEAST, YE DO IT UNTO ME."

THE SUBSTANCE OF THIS VOLUME
WAS GIVEN AS THE
EARLE LECTURES
AT THE
PACIFIC THEOLOGICAL SEMINARY
IN
1907

CONTENTS

CHAPTER I
PHILOSOPHY AND THE SOCIAL QUESTION . . . . PAGE 1

CHAPTER II
SOCIAL SCIENCE, SOCIOLOGY, AND THE SOCIAL QUESTION . 28

CHAPTER III
ECONOMICS AND THE SOCIAL QUESTION 53

CHAPTER IV
ETHICS AND THE SOCIAL QUESTION 96

CHAPTER V
ETHICAL IDEALISM AND THE SOCIAL QUESTION . . . 136

CHAPTER VI
RELIGION AND THE SOCIAL QUESTION 165

INDEX 205

THE APPROACH TO THE SOCIAL QUESTION

I

PHILOSOPHY AND THE SOCIAL QUESTION

AT the end of his brilliant book on the philosophy of society[1] Professor Stein remarks that as the fifteenth century had for its task the renaissance of art, and the sixteenth century the reformation of religion, and the seventeenth century the development of science, and the eighteenth century the promotion of democracy, so the task of the twentieth century is to be the reformation and reconstruction of the social world. "A new renaissance," he says, "must break upon the modern world, a deliverance from the gloom of pessimism which is the symptom of an overworked and weary period; a transformation of the instincts of social evolution into rational laws; a quickening of the glad and confident service of the social world, as it is and as it is to be." Such a prophecy may well appear too restricted to cover the infinitely varied

[1] Stein, "Die soziale Frage im Lichte der Philosophie," 1897, s. 773. The abbreviated ed., 1903, omits the passage.

life of the twentieth century. Other problems are pressing besides that of social redemption. The interests and aims of human society are too complex to be reduced to a single formula. Art, if not so creative as in the fifteenth century, seems likely to receive fresh appreciation; religion, if not so authoritative as in the sixteenth century, is at least more widely applied; democracy, if not so buoyantly trusted as in the eighteenth century, must be redeemed by more democracy. The coming century is perhaps quite as likely to be remembered for its appropriation and application of inherited ideals, as for its exclusive concern for a newly discovered aim.

Yet, even if one may hesitate to prophesy about a century, he can hardly be mistaken as to his own generation and time. The foreground of immediate interest is unquestionably held by the needs and problems of the social world. Never before were so many people concerned with the amelioration of social conditions and the realization of social dreams. The most conspicuous and disturbing fact of contemporary life is its social unrest. No institution of society — the family, the state, or the church — is so fixed in stability or in sanctity as to be safe from radical transformation. The growth of the great industry, with its combinations of capital and its organizations of labor, the unprecedented accumulation of wealth in the hands of the few, and the equally unprecedented increase of power in the hands of the many, — these, and many other signs of the time, point to new social adjustments, and awaken a new social spirit. It is the age of the Social Question; and those who have embarked on enterprises of social service and social reformation feel beneath their little ventures the sustaining movement of the main current of the time. Art, if it is to flourish, must concern itself with the problems of the common life and contribute to the happiness and solace of the masses of men; religion, if it is to control modern life, must add to its ministry to the single soul the redemption of the social world; and democracy, having won its political victory, has now before it a further conflict with feudalism, paternalism, and privilege entrenched in their industrial strongholds. The ideals of other ages — æsthetic, religious, and political — find themselves reproduced and comprehended in the new ideal of a better world which marks the age of the Social Question.

It is inevitable that the first response to this new ideal should be that of action, experiment, and relief. Here are social evils to be uprooted, social maladies to be cured, social wrongs to be righted, and the heart of the time leaps to meet this demand with quickly summoned resources of compassion, indignation, sympathy, and hope. Here, at the same time, is the best of opportunities for the precipitate, emotional, or self-confident counsellor; for heat to be substituted for light, and sentiment for science. The man with a panacea for social ills is sure of a welcome. "If my plan is not satisfactory," said one such reformer, "what is yours?"—as though any self-respecting citizen must carry about his person a scheme of social redemption. Social surgery is to the impatient practitioner more tempting than the slow processes of social prevention and social hygiene. "When I am in doubt," a young physician is reported to have said, "I generally operate for appendicitis." Modern social life, however, is too intricate an organism to provide good clinical material for careless experimentation. Antecedent to wise social practice there is needed a better social diagnosis. Before the Social Question can be answered, it must be understood. Before social diseases can be exterminated, social pathology must discover the nature and causes of epidemic distress.

There is, no doubt, a risk in academic neutrality and moral timidity, and bold experiment may be more profitable than cautious inaction; yet, the more one realizes the dimensions and complexity of the Social Question, the more he becomes impressed with the necessity of a well-considered plan of attack. A frontal charge on social ills may be like the charge at Balaclava, magnificent, but not war. Modern battles are, for the most part, determined, not on the field, but in the studies of the General Staff. Indeed, the Social Question is so varied and so recurrent, that a complete answer to it may be as unattainable as the complete extirpation of physical disease. The Social Question is not so much a problem to be solved as a campaign to be organized and directed, a process to be interpreted, accelerated, and checked. It is as fluid and changeful, and often as turbid and violent, as a rushing stream. It is a contemporary expression of social evolution, perpetually varying in form as the current of thought is swept through the channel of time. To look for a solution of the Social Question is, therefore, to expect a hurrying stream to stand still or to run dry. An answer to the Social Question is like an answer to life. It assumes that life is a fixed fact, when it is in reality a fact in motion. The meaning of life shifts with its moving desires. The problem of childhood is not the problem of manhood. To read the riddle of life one must run as he reads. To catch the present moment one must catch it on the wing. It is the same with the Social Question. "When any one brings forward a solution," one of the most observant of American students once remarked, "I move to adjourn." The approach to the Social Question is like the approach to the North Pole. A prudent explorer does not expect to arrive by a dash; he plans relay-parties, some of which must support the one which may succeed. Many ways of approach must be tried that one may be found. "Only a world-history," a distinguished German teacher has said, "can answer a world-problem."[1]

At such a time then, what is it which the Social Question most imperatively needs? It needs, as

[1] Ziegler, "Die soziale Frage eine ethische Frage," 1891, s. 7.

always, fresh accessions of zeal and warmer co-operation of sympathy; but it needs still more a new quality of sanity, wisdom, patience, and insight; the steadying and directing of social action by general principles or laws. In other words, the Social Question is waiting for a philosophy. In Mr. Lowes Dickinson's "Modern Symposium" one of the disputants gives his estimate of the American character: "The future for them is the kingdom of elevators, telephones, motor cars, and flying machines. . . . The principle of the universe is Acceleration. . . . We do not know whence we come, or whither we go, and what is more important, we do not care; what we do know is that we are moving faster than any one ever moved before." What is thus described as Americanism may be affirmed of much social reform. It does not know whither it is moving, but it is moving very fast. Precisely as the commercial world is tempted by the doctrine: "Get rich, quick!" so the social world is tempted by the corresponding doctrine: "Do good, quick!" and the fruits of this doctrine are zeal without knowledge, generosity without discrimination, discontent without discernment. Acceleration becomes a substitute for reflection; precipitancy supplants efficiency; and the worst recreancy to duty is to stop and think. It seems a good time, then, to pause and reconsider the nature of the problem which underlies the facts of social agitation and discontent. The force which they carry is like a high-power electric current, which must either be insulated or work disaster. Social stability, like the City of God, must have foundations. Social navigation needs a chart of the course. Much social teaching shows the channel by the wrecks of ventures which have missed it. "Do you know all the rocks in this harbor?" asks the captain. "Every one," answers the pilot, and as the vessel at that moment strikes, he adds: "There is one of them now."

It may be objected that to interrupt social action by the reconsideration of social theory is to retreat from the task of the present age to an earlier world of social speculations and dreams; that the days of social theorizing are past and the day of social service has arrived. It must be remembered, however, that theory and practice are not alternatives from which one has to choose. The theorist is not the run-away from action, or the stay-at-home in a moral war. Theory, in its Greek signification, is the beholding of things as they are. The theorist is the spectator at the game of life, who sees its parts in their proportions and relations. He has detachment and horizon; the details of his problem take their place in a general view. "He sees things steadily and sees them whole." The theorist is like the commander who stands apart from the fighting, but directs the battle and foresees its end. The army accomplishes what the theorist has planned. Has not this detached view of things its place in the Social Question? Doers there are in plenty, but where are the seers? Sympathy, sacrifice, loyalty, compassion, all these are freely dedicated; but where are the antecedent qualities of sanity, grasp, and insight? However imperfectly these gifts may be attained, are they not worth the seeking? May not social enthusiasm march with firmer step if social philosophy has cleared the way?

These considerations appear to justify one in turning briefly from the fascinating occupation of solving the Social Question to the more modest task of understanding the Social Question. What kind of question is this which thus confronts the modern world? Is it possible to stand back from its details and survey it as a whole? May not a very large and complex question be easily mistaken for a small and easy one? Where, among the philosophies which interpret human life, shall one find an open door into the nature of the Social Question? Is there such a door, or must one grope his way in the dark? What common character unites these infinitely varied forms of social service and desire? What has the Social Question to gain from philosophy; and what has philosophy to give to the Social Question?

In order to answer these questions, it is necessary to recall, in the most general and preliminary way, first, the meaning and scope of the Social Question, and, secondly, the purpose and method of philosophy.

The Social Question, in its most elementary

form, is approached when one becomes aware among the problems of conduct that he is not alone, but a person among other persons, a member of the social order, a part of a social whole. Self-realization, as the philosophers would say, must then be sought, not apart from others, but in relation to others. The problems of life which had seemed personal become social problems. The ethics of self-development become social ethics.

When one enumerates the various sciences which propose to interpret human life, there present themselves, in the first place, a series which appear to deal with the individual as though he were alone. Physiology examines the individual as body; logic, the individual as mind; psychology, the correlation of mind and body in the individual; ethics, the duty of the person; metaphysics, the ideals of the person. All these inquiries seem to detach the person from the mass, as though he occupied a little universe of his own. Robinson Crusoe, in the solitude of his island, had at his command, it would seem, not only the leisure but also the material for composing a learned treatise on any one of these sciences. He had as companions his body, his mind, and his conscience; and many a busy author might sigh for so admirable an opportunity to compile without interruption his text-book on logic, or psychology, or ethics, if only he might hope that the footprint on the sand were that of a friendly publisher.

Is this apparent detachment of the individual,

however, real? On the contrary, such a person, thus completely detached from other persons, does not in fact exist. One may theoretically abstract the problems of his body, or mind, or will, from the world of other people and contemplate them as isolated facts; but in reality one does not and cannot thus live. The universe of the isolated self is an imaginary universe. By the very conditions of human infancy one is born, not alone, but into a community of three: his parents and himself. Nor does he live alone, but in a group, a village, a clan, a town, a university, a nation. The name he bears indicates his descent, his race, his social tradition. Man is a social animal. "Never in human history, except in sporadic instances, have completely segregated lives been found. Man belongs to the herding animals."[1] Robinson Crusoe may appear to himself completely alone, and his solitude creates for him the pathos of his fate. But what makes him able to endure this solitude? It is the recollection of the social order to which he belongs, and the hope of restoration to the social world. Though alone, he is a social being. His body is a product of social heredity; his mind is stocked with memories of his country and home; his hopes bind him to the social order; the footprint on the sand is the symbol of a social world.

Thus the Social Question invades even those sciences which appear to be concerned with the

[1] Schmoller, "Grundriss der allgemeinen Volkswirtschaftslehre," 1900, erster Teil, s. 7.

single life. Physiology may study the body of the individual, but that body is the product of ages of social history, and becomes the symbol of the social heredity and environment from which it has sprung. Logic may concern itself with the order of one's own thought, but that order of thought is the product of centuries of intellectual development, of which the individual mind is a witness and expression. Metaphysics may concern itself with personal ideals, but these personal problems are inextricably involved in the larger unity of a social idealism, and open into a doctrine, not of the soul of the person alone, but of the soul of the world. All problems of human life are parts of the Social Question. "The *ego* and the *alter* are thus born together. . . . Both *ego* and *alter* are thus essentially social; each is a *socius*."[1] "A separate individual is an abstraction unknown to experience."[2] The Social Question is, in a word, the outer margin of the question of personal experience: "Set, as I inevitably am, within the social order, how shall my own life be realized, amplified, sustained, and serviceable therein?"

The testimony of the loftiest minds in the history of human thought confirms this general statement of the Social Question. The adjustment of the person to the social order was, for example, the central theme of Greek philosophy. Plato's

[1] Baldwin, "Mental Development in the Child and Race," 3d ed., 1906, p. 321.
[2] Cooley, "Human Nature and the Social Order," 1902, p. 1.

"Republic" was based on the correspondence between the nature of an individual and the nature of a State. What the reason, the will, and the passions were in the one, the councillors, the soldiers, and the masses were in the other. The harmonious soul was the counterpart of the well-ordered State. Plato, as his English editor remarks, "identifies the individual and the State, ethics with politics. He thinks that most of a State which is most like one man, and in which the citizens have the greatest uniformity of character."[1] Aristotle's "Politics" also, though less concerned with social idealism,[2] is not less explicit in its social philosophy. "Man is by nature a political animal. And he, who by nature and not by mere accident is without a State, is either above humanity, or below it. . . . The individual, when isolated, is not self-sufficing; and therefore he is like a part in relation to the whole. But he who is unable to live in society, or who has no need because he is sufficient for himself, must be either a beast or a god."[3] Thus, as one of the most eminent of English scholars has said, "To the common consciousness of Greece the State or the City was not an organization but an organism. . . . It was the individual

---

[1] Jowett, Introduction to "Republic," "The Dialogues of Plato," 1871, II, p. 150.

[2] Mr. Lowell went so far as to say that: "To a mind more interested in the soul of things than in the body, the little finger of Plato is thicker than the loins of Aristotle." "Literary Essays," 1892, IV, p. 252.

[3] "Politics," tr. Jowett, 1885, I, p. 4.

on his ideal side; his true and spiritual self; . . . the higher unity in which he merged his separate or selfish self. . . '. Only through the social organism could each part, by adaptation to the others, develop its inherent powers."[1]

What Greek philosophy thus expressed in the language of politics, Christian theology soon reiterated in the language of religion. The Apostle Paul appropriated to his new faith the Greek teaching which he had received, and pictured the Church of Christ as a living body with its interdependent parts. "The body is not one member, but many. . . . The eye cannot say unto the hand, I have no need of thee. . . . They are many members, but one body. . . . Now ye are the body of Christ and severally members thereof."[2] The individual, in other words, finds his own vitality in his relation to the social whole. Cut off from the common life his own life becomes withered and atrophied. He lives as he serves. He finds life as he loses it. The Pauline doctrine of social service was a Greek translation of the Hebrew idealism which Jesus inherited and spiritualized in his teaching of the Kingdom of God. Clothed as this hope of Jesus necessarily was in the eschatological language which alone made it intelligible to his hearers, and colored as his own thoughts may have been by the prevailing anticipation of a supernatural and apocalyptic kingdom, it was

[1] Butcher, "Some Aspects of the Greek Genius," 1891, p. 51.
[2] 1 Cor. xii. 12 ff.

none the less a social ideal which hovered before his mind, the dream of a regenerated and organic humanity in which the scattered lives of men should find their unity in the service of God.[1]

The scope of the Social Question is thus no new discovery. Round the problem of the individual, like an ocean environing an island, the greatest of spiritual teachers have seen the larger circle of social relations and needs which the individual is called to master and explore. Yet though this truth of the social nature of man has never been without its witnesses, it has received such fresh momentum from the circumstances of modern life as to become a practically new force in contemporary thought. Within the memory of persons still living there has occurred this transition from a philosophy bounded by the individual to a philosophy covering the social order. The word "Coöperation" applied to industrial life is said to have originated with Robert Owen as late as 1821[2]; the word "Sociology" was coined, it is believed, by Comte about 1839,[3] and the phrase "the Social Organism" was popularized for English readers by Herbert Spencer in 1860.[4]

---

[1] Cf. Peabody, "Christian Eschatology and Christian Ethics," *Harvard Theological Review*, January, 1909.

[2] "The Social Economist," August 27, 1821: "THE SECRET IS OUT: it is unrestrained COÖPERATION, on the part of ALL the members, for EVERY purpose of social life." Holyoake, "The History of Coöperation," 1906, I, p. 40.

[3] Cf. Ch. II, p. 46.

[4] *Westminster Review*, January, 1860, "The Social Organism."

Many influences conspired to delay this transition. The Christian religion had made its original appeal to the individual and had given a new value to the single soul. The first discovery of Jesus Christ, it has been said, was the discovery of personality. The shepherd sought the one sheep; the woman swept the house for the one lost coin. No life was so insignificant or unworthy as to forfeit its value in the sight of God. The poor, the slave, the stranger, the sinner, — all had their part in the great redemption. Protestantism reiterated the same truth, affirming the right of individual judgment and the spiritual dignity of the single soul. English jurisprudence perpetuated the same tradition. "The unit of an ancient society," it was pointed out, "was the Family, of a modern society the Individual."[1] Ethics reënforced the same view. Its classical text-books analyzed the consciousness of the individual, inquiring how many virtues, passions, or vices a human life normally contained. Religion, also, was a gift to the individual, and the salvation of the single soul was the sufficient end of God's grace.

With the coming of the modern world and its miracles of intercommunication and interdependence, a new interpretation of individual life has become a necessity of rational thought. The unity of the world is no longer a pleasant dream, but a demonstrated fact. Each incident of trade or

[1] Maine, "Ancient Law," ed. Pollock, 4th Amer. ed., 1906, p. 121.

event of politics or catastrophe of nature — a crop in Montana, a war in China, or an earthquake in Italy — affects the welfare, stimulates the production, or stirs the sympathy, of people on the other side of the globe. The preciousness of the individual is not forfeited in this larger view. The person remains the centre of economic, or moral, or religious concern. Out from the efficiency of individuals radiate the social forces of the world; but the circle within which personality may operate, the range of its opportunity, responsibility, and effect, the social expansion of individual capacity, has become recognized by the thought of the present age, as it has not been appreciated since Aristotle defined man as a social animal, and Jesus Christ came into Galilee preaching the Gospel of the Kingdom of God.

What is the new note in modern jurisprudence? It is the determination of rights and duties within the social order of the community, the nation, or the world. With what does modern legislation concern itself? It deals in an unparalleled degree with the obligations of associated individuals, with combinations of industry, with functions of government, with adjustments of economic and domestic life. What is modern ethics? It is no longer an enumeration of the virtues and vices of the individual, but an inquiry how the good man may make the better world. And what is modern religion? One of the most characteristic books of the present generation has for its title: "The World as the

Subject of Redemption."[1] It is a phrase which could hardly have occurred to an author fifty years ago. Modern religion has for its subject, not the individual detached from the world, but the world itself in whose redemption the individual has his share.

Finally, the new habit of mind is expressed in a single phrase, which has already become a commonplace of modern speech, but which a generation ago had the appearance of novelty, if not of radicalism. "Is society an organism?" asked Herbert Spencer, in one of his earliest essays,[2] and he proceeded to enumerate the likenesses and the unlikenesses to physical forms which social groupings exhibit. There has remained, it is true, much room for debate between the biologists and the psychologists as to the precise answer to the question; but whatever conclusion may be reached concerning the nature of society, whether it be regarded as a physical form or a psychical process, or as "physico-psychic, — a psychical organism, but with a physical basis,"[3] — the fundamental confession is in all cases the same. Social life, whatever its specific character may be, is not a disconnected series of incidental events, but the unfolding of a continuous unity,

---

[1] Fremantle, "The World as the Subject of Redemption," Bampton Lectures of 1883, 2d ed., 1895.

[2] Reprinted in "Essays, Scientific, Political, and Speculative," London, 1868, I, p. 384; and again in "Illustrations of Universal Progress," N. Y., 1870, p. 384.

[3] Giddings, "Principles of Sociology," 1896, p. 420.

whose total progress and destiny each part may promote or retard. What to the Apostle Paul was a prophetic dream has thus become a scientific fact. We are members one of another, and no part of the social body can say of another: I have no need of thee. The meaning of each part is discovered as it fulfils its function in the whole. The problem of each life is to serve the whole. The conception of the Social Organism gives security and significance to the life of each social atom. It is a transition in thought which can be compared with nothing less than the transition in astronomy, when the Ptolemaic conception of the universe was supplanted by the Copernican conception, and the earth, which had seemed the centre of a system, was discovered to have its orbit as one of many planets round a larger sun. So the philosophy of individualism, with its Ptolemaic conception of the individual life, is supplanted by the philosophy of the social order, where the individual finds himself within the Copernican system of a larger world.

Such is the spacious region where the person, finding himself environed and developed by the world of other people, meets the Social Question. "Life," said Mazzini in one of his noblest utterances, "is one; the individual and society are its two necessary manifestations. . . . We cannot suppress or subalternize one without irreparably mutilating our power. . . . Truth is found at their point of intersection."[1] What, then, is the question which

[1] "Essays," Camelot Series, 1887, p. 286.

meets the individual as he thus finds himself at this point of intersection with the social life? It is the question of adjustment between these two factors of experience, the individual and the social whole. How to maintain each without sacrificing the other; how to be a person and at the same time an efficient member of the social body; how to realize personality in terms of the common good, — this, in its many forms of statement, is the Social Question. It may be asked in terms of the family, where a man or a woman, conscious of individual rights, is at the same time a member of a group whose stability depends on sacrifice and service. It may be asked in terms of philanthropy, where giver and receiver seem set apart in their conditions and needs, but find themselves associated in the organic intimacy of a community or a State. It may be asked in terms of the industrial order, where employer and employed have their distinct functions to perform, while the total movement of economic life holds them in its service. Wherever the incompleteness of the isolated life becomes plain, and the problem of self-realization is seen in the setting of the common good, there, out of this social consciousness, issues the Social Question — the problem of self-adjustment to society, the desire to harmonize one's own ideal with the ideal of a better world.

Here, also, enters the sense of impatience, even of tragedy, which so often attends the Social Question. For this adjustment between the parts and the whole is never complete; the Social Question is never fully answered; the individual and the social order march at unequal pace; the rights of the one outrun or lag behind those of the other. There ensues maladjustment, suffering, misunderstanding, conflict. Thus, the Social Question represents the gradual evolution of a stable society; it is the Peace-Movement of the modern world, forever unrealized, and to many minds Utopian, yet steadily modifying the conduct and the ideals of the time. The absolute adjustment of the person to the social order is the final social synthesis, foreshadowed by many experiments, but to be fully realized only when the completely developed person meets the completely consistent world, and the two are perfected in one.

If such, in the most general terms, is the comprehensive intention of the Social Question, how shall it be philosophically approached? Is there any principle of conduct which may admit one to its interpretation? What is the philosophy of the Social Question? To answer this question one must begin with another. What is philosophy? How shall philosophy be distinguished from other kinds of knowledge? What is it to philosophize? Much superfluous difficulty has been met at this point by students of philosophy, as though the subject of philosophy were peculiarly esoteric or abstract. It has been, on the one hand, held that philosophy differs from other knowledge in what philosophers call its form;

and again it has been taught that philosophy differs from other knowledge in what philosophers call its content. Philosophy, in the first case, would offer a special way to knowledge, or, in the second case, would contain a special sort of knowledge.

The first of these alternatives assumes that philosophy reaches truth by a special road. Other knowledge, it is suggested, is reached by observation, by experience, by empirical methods; philosophy proceeds by introspection, intuition, *à priori* methods. Science observes, philosophy speculates. In our common knowledge we walk by sight; in philosophy we walk by faith. Are these two ways of knowledge, however, alternatives from which one must choose? On the contrary, all knowledge is gained by the joint use of both ways of approach. All knowledge begins in observation, and is analyzed and clarified by reflection. Observation without reflection may see, but it does not understand. As the Apostle James says, it is like a man beholding his face in a glass, and straightway forgetting what manner of man he is. Reflection, on the other hand, without observation, is at the mercy of the unobserved facts; and many a would-be philosopher has thus been powerless in the presence of reality. When Mr. Lowell, in the homely language of the " Biglow Papers," says of such a man that —

> " He comes bunt up agin a fect
> And goes to pieces when he ought'er ect,"

he is but repeating the dictum of Kant: "Without the senses no object would be given to us; without the understanding no object would be thought. Thoughts without content are empty; intuitions without conceptions are blind."[1] One may, that is to say, look and yet not see, because he does not think; or one may think and yet not know, because he does not look. A mind without ideas, though it observes, is blind; an idea which is not observed is empty. To see, and to reflect on what one sees, constitutes the reaction of the mind on its environment. There can be, therefore, no distinction of "form" between philosophical knowledge and other ways of knowledge. The only distinction possible is between good thinking and bad thinking, between observation which is blind and ideas which are empty. "Contemplation," said Owen Feltham, in his "Resolves," "generates; action propagates. Without the first the latter is defective, without the last the first is but abortive and embryonic. . . . I will neither always be busy and doing, nor ever shut up in nothing but thought." We think, that is to say, as we walk: one side at a time; but the balanced action of both sides gives poise to the motion alike of the body and of the mind.

Can it be maintained, on the other hand, that philosophy differs from other kinds of knowledge in its content? Other knowledge, it may seem, is concerned with outward facts or concrete realities,

[1] "Kritik der reinen Vernunft," ed. Hartenstein, 1868, III, s. 82.

while philosophy deals with spiritual experiences or ideal aims. This distinction appears more plausible than that of form. Science, it is true, is for the most part occupied with physical facts, and philosophy is for the most part concerned with spiritual truths. Yet the outward and the inward, the spiritual and the physical, are so inextricably involved in all experience that no boundary can be rigidly drawn between the two. One of the most interesting of modern vocations, for example, is that of physiological psychology, with its equipment of laboratories and instruments of precision to measure and analyze the operations of the mind or will. Is such a study to be classified as philosophical or scientific? Is it concerned with material facts or with spiritual facts? Is it a part of physics or a part of metaphysics? It is all of these at once. It applies the tests of physical science to the facts of spiritual experience. Emotions, habits, and instincts are measured in terms of motion, time-reaction, and effort. The very existence of this new pursuit, with its dramatic results in the interpretation of consciousness, quite obliterates the line between the study of the spiritual and the study of the physical. Philosophy must comprehend all sorts of facts. The world as a whole is the subject of philosophy. Neither in form nor in content is philosophy to be distinguished from other ways of approaching truth.

What, then, is philosophy, and how shall any subject be philosophically pursued? Philosophy is, in fact, a much simpler thing than the technical language and subtle methods of some philosophers would appear to suggest. Philosophy is nothing else than the summing up one's knowledge, the unification of one's thinking, the comprehension of scattered truths under a common principle or law. It is the best one knows about any subject of which he thinks, the summary of his reflection and experience. Truths are segments; philosophy is the circle of truth. Truths are diverse; Truth is one. Truths divide, confuse, restrict; but the Truth, as the Fourth Gospel says, makes men free.

This was the sane idea of philosophy which prevailed among the Greeks. The philosopher, Plato taught, "is a lover, not of a part of wisdom only, but of the whole . . . a lover of the sight of truth. . . . And to these, when perfected by years and education, and to these only, you will intrust the State."[1] There is a tradition, repeated by Cicero, of a visit of Pythagoras to the city of Phlius. Being asked by the Prince concerning the art to which he devoted himself, he answered that he professed no art, and was simply a philosopher. The Prince inquired wherein a philosopher differed from other men, and Pythagoras replied that human life seemed to resemble a great fair, to which some resorted to buy and sell, and others simply to look about them. "These, then, are they whom I call

[1] "Republic," V, 475, 487, tr. Jowett, 1871, pp. 309, 320.

students of wisdom, for such is meant by philosopher."[1] Thus the philosopher sees, as it were, all that is going on. He has, as Robert Louis Stevenson said of Jesus Christ, "not so much views, as a *view*." He stands where facts fall into their place, and are seen in perspective and proportion. Philosophy is not a dogma, but a habit of mind; not a creed, but an attitude of the spirit. "Philosophy is really only a particularly determined attempt to follow out the path of knowledge or experience. . . . Culture which takes itself seriously tends to become philosophy."[2] "Philosophy, in other words, mistakes its place when it sets itself up as a dogmatic system of life. Its function is to comprehend, and from comprehension to criticise, and through criticising to unify."[3] "Philosophy is . . . the deepening and broadening of the common practical thoughtfulness. . . . Between the fitful or prudential thinking of some little man of affairs, and the sustained thought of the devoted lover of truth, there is indeed a long journey, but it is a straight journey along the same road."[4]

If, then, this is the task of philosophy; if it is a journey along the same road which all thinking takes, steadily pursued until the meaning of things

---

[1] Cicero, "Tusc. Quæst.," lib. v, c. 3, cited by Sir Wm. Hamilton, "Lectures on Metaphysics," 1859, I, p. 46.

[2] Muirhead, "Philosophy and Life," 1902, pp. 19, 10.

[3] Wallace, "Hegel's Philosophy of Mind," 1894, p. cxxxviii.

[4] Perry, "The Approach to Philosophy," 1905, pp. 21, 22.

is explored; how shall such a way of insight be found to the interpretation of the social world? Where is the high-road to a philosophy of the Social Question? Here are these scattered problems: the family, philanthropy, industrial life, racial division and collision. How shall a particularly determined attempt be made to reach their meaning and unity? Is there beneath these varied forms of social action any common intention or desire? Is it possible to attain not merely views of them, but a view? Through what gate of thought may one enter most immediately into the meaning of modern social life? What is the key which opens this gate and lets one in? In answer to these questions there present themselves four ways of approach, which appear to lead toward a philosophy of the Social Question. Like the City of God in the Book of Revelation, the Social Question lies four-square, and toward each front leads a well-travelled road. Each of these four approaches to the Social Question has been trodden by many students, and there are aspects of the Social Question which may be best seen from each of these converging roads. The first of these approaches is by the way of social science; the second is by the way of sociology; the third is by the way of economics; the fourth is by the way of ethics. By any one of these ways one may journey with many companions toward the interpretation of the Social Question, and hear along the road the varied and tumultuous noises of the time. At what point, then, may one hope to arrive as he takes up the march along each of these four roads? What degree of insight, what right of entrance does he gain? By what way does he enter most directly through the gate into the city?

II

SOCIAL SCIENCE, SOCIOLOGY, AND THE SOCIAL QUESTION

THE most obvious and open way which offers itself as an approach to the Social Question — and one which has invited and rewarded many minds — is the way known as Social Science. The National Association for the Promotion of Social Science was founded in England in 1857 under the leadership of Lord Brougham; the *Association Internationale pour le Progrès des Sciences Sociales* was organized in France in 1862; the American Social Science Association was established in 1865; and the *Journal of Social Science*, the organ of the American Association, was first issued in June, 1869, and is still an important annual review of social progress.[1]

Historically, therefore, social science was the way of approach first selected by modern students. This approach has the further merit of announcing without ambiguity the method of research which must be consistently applied to the Social Question. Social science pledges its students to apply to

[1] *Journal of Social Science*, I, p. 10, Villard, "A Historical Sketch."

social facts the scientific method. And what is the scientific method? There are three steps by which the student of science proceeds, and which, as they are taken in succession, mark the development of the scientific mind. The first problem of science is that of accurate and scrupulous observation. The geologist observes the stratification of the rocks; the historian explores the evidence of documents; the chemist analyzes the elements and combinations of the material world. Lectures on science are not the most essential part of the scientific method. Not the ear, but the eye, is the primary organ of education in science; and next to the eye the hand. The laboratory, the dissecting table, the clinic, the microscope, the museum, are the chief instruments of scientific learning. The great apostle of the scientific method in education, the discoverer that science is concerned with facts rather than with words, was Mr. Squeers. "C-l-e-a-n," he said, "clean, to make bright, to scour; W-i-n-d-e-r, a casement. When the boy knows this out of book, he goes and does it."

This step in the method of science is as applicable to the facts of social life as to the facts of nature. Scattered before one in the modern world are the varied incidents which create the Social Question — wealth and poverty, employment and unemployment, drink and crime, social reform and social service, the stratification of social classes, the sources of social discontent, the elements and combinations of industrial life; and the first demand laid on the student of these facts is to see them precisely as they are, to escape from an unreal, visionary, Utopian world, and to recognize the actual conditions and tendencies of the world as it is. Nothing is more familiar in social history than the ingenious structures of schemes and dreams, which were built, not on the rock of fact, but on the sands of sentiment, and in the first storm of practical experiment were sure to fall. Social science holds the student to the solid ground. It is the field-work of the Social Question, the application to social facts of the inductive method. The first step in social wisdom is the acquisition of this scientific habit of mind, which is in reality nothing more than a patient, alert, and dispassionate common-sense. "The roots of the scientific spirit," it has been lately said by a distinguished man of science, "are in an unconditional desire for the truth, an incorruptible judgment, a delight in logical thinking, thoroughness, and the willingness to go slow."[1]

Among the provisions which contribute to this scientific observation of social facts, the most novel is the collection of material in a Social Museum. Natural science has long recognized that such collections, even on the most extensive and expensive scale, are indispensable to scientific progress; and the time seems to have arrived when social movements may exhibit the same world-wide distribution and variety

[1] Klein, "Wissenschaft und Technik," Int. Wochenschrift, 2ter Jahrg., No. 42, October, 1908.

which makes a museum of natural history an essential instrument of instruction. The facts of philanthropy, industry, poor-relief, housing, insurance, coöperation, alcoholism, and penology are as capable of graphic representation as the life and habits of beetles or plants. To set together these scattered and often unfamiliar types of social procedure, and to lay before the student the total experience of the world in various forms of social service, is not only to inform the observer concerning his special task, but to impress him with the scope of the Social Question and to send him back to his own work with a sense of background, enlargement, and hope. A Social Museum is the best of remedies for provincialism in social action, for the self-deception of originality, for ignorance of precedents or parallels, and for the superfluous imitation of methods which have been already tried and discarded by the experience of the world.

To the step of observation in the training of the scientific mind succeeds the second step of generalization. The collecting of facts is preliminary to the comparison of facts. A museum of natural history is not established to amuse sightseers, but to provide material for scientific generalization. A man of science once remarked that his intellectual problem was to convert his mind into a mirror which should reflect facts. Observation, accurate and immediate, like the image in a mirror, seemed to him the end of science. But does this habit of mind adequately represent the scientific spirit? On the contrary, it indicates with precision the difference between a small man of science and a great man of science. To a small man of science the mind is a mirror which reflects facts, but is not penetrated by them. The great man of science not only sees the facts, but sees into them. He has not only sight, but insight. He not only observes, but generalizes. The facts speak, and the mind answers. The generalization may indeed outrun the facts, as though the reflecting mirror threw its light behind the facts which it received, and invited observation to verify or dissipate the shadowy suggestions dimly seen. Science, in a word, permits not only precision, but imagination. The test of the great mind applied to nature is its capacity for thoroughly controlled and effectively applied guesswork. The army of science marches behind the scouts of hypothesis, who may often fall back defeated, but who none the less clear the way. "Without principles," it has been forcibly said, in a remarkable book, "which at every stage transcend precise confirmation through such experience as is then accessible, the organization of experience is impossible." [1]

This transition, also, from observation to generalization, is not less practicable and inviting in the study of social facts than in the study of physical

[1] Poincaré, "Science and Hypothesis," tr. Halsted, 1905, Introduction by Royce, p. xxiii.

facts. Observation sets before one a disconnected series of industrial, political, racial, or philanthropic incidents, and social science proceeds to inquire whether these scattered facts indicate any general principle which gives to these varied enterprises and schemes a common character. Does comparison discover analogies of purpose and plan which suggest a unity of origin or aim? May sight be quickened by insight, and precision be reënforced by imagination? Here is the further significance of a Social Museum. By the very diversity of types which it offers for observation it may suggest the right direction of reform, the least obstructed line of progress, the relation of social action to different social traditions or opportunities, and the line of social evolution which these varied facts appear to confirm. Social Utopias, coöperative experiments, industrial insurance, plans of housing, social settlements, liquor legislation, the experience of many lands and many periods, all lie before the observer as material for a comparative estimate of applicability, practicability, and utility, under the special conditions of his own time and place. The comparative method excludes the accidental, discovers the essential, and indicates as accurately in social science as in natural science the prevailing type.[1]

Yet even at this point the scientific method has

[1] Cf. Peabody, "The Social Museum as an Instrument of University Teaching," Pub. of the Dep. of Social Ethics in Harvard Univ., No. 1, 1908.

not taken its most dramatic step. Experiment and comparison, observation and generalization, suggest to the scientific mind not only the infinite diversity of the facts observed and the coördinating principles which they illustrate, but beneath all these partial generalizations the profounder truth of an underlying unity in nature. No transition in the history of science has been so momentous as that which occurred through the discovery of the conservation of energy. Heat, light, motion, electricity — these, which had been studied as separable and isolated modes of action, became infinitely more significant when seen to be transformable and correlated in the marvellous unity of the physical world. "Everywhere throughout the Cosmos," to use Mr. Spencer's words, "this truth must invariably hold. Every successive change or group of changes going on in it, must be due to forces affiliable on the like or unlike force previously existing; while from the forces exhibited in such change or changes must be derived others more or less transformed."[1]

The student of social science applies these words to his own theme and observes the same conservation of energy operating among social forces. There, also, each successive change is due to forces previously existing, and leads to other forces more or less transformed. The various social movements, which at first appeared so distinguishable and isolated — the problems of the family, of

[1] "First Principles," 1869, p. 202.

poverty, of industry, of drink — each with its own literature, experiments, programmes, and solutions, are yet correlated expressions of the unity of the social world.[1] No sooner does the inquirer touch one of these subjects, than he finds it converted into another, as motion is converted into heat, and electricity into light or motion. He approaches, for example, the problem of the family, its historical evolution and its contemporary perils; but as this problem is scrutinized it discloses within itself a series of further problems, which are apparently not concerned with the family, but with other tendencies and perils of modern life. Where shall one look for the causes of instability in the modern family? Are they to be found in circumstances of poverty, in bad housing, congested living, and the recklessness of lives that have lost their hope? Then the problem of the family becomes at once correlated with the problem of judicious poor-relief, and the integrity of the family becomes dependent on social action concerning the city, the saloon, and the slum. Or, on the other hand, is the phenomenon of instability in the family due to the demoralization of prosperity? Does domestic looseness occur quite as often among the rich as among the poor? Then the problem of the family becomes correlated with the tendency to social restlessness and self-indul-

[1] Cf. Peabody, "Jesus Christ and the Social Question," 1900, Ch. VII: "The Correlation of the Social Questions," where the analogy is treated in greater detail.

gence, and is but one aspect of the extravagance, laxity, and degeneration which afflict the commercialized and materialized rich.

The same correlation meets one at each step among the social questions. One of the most impressive facts, for example, discovered by the scientific study of poverty, both in the United States and in Great Britain, is the fact that the causes of destitution which must be referred to misfortune as their cause outnumber the causes due to misconduct in the proportion of two to one.[1] Poverty, that is to say, is in this degree a consequence of intermittent employment, sickness, old age, or death, rather than of personal delinquency; and charity, detached from this appreciation of its industrial and physical causes, becomes extravagant, ineffective, or cruel.

A striking instance of this interplay of varied causes and effects is provided by the housing-problem. In one aspect it is a part of the problem of the family; but it is at the same time a contribution to the problem of industry and an essential factor in the promotion of economic efficiency. Unsanitary and congested living diminishes the economic product and increases economic waste. Thus the better housing of wage-earners has come to be recognized by wise employers, not primarily as a question of philanthropy, or even as a contribution to domestic integrity, but as a legitimate part of judicious business, diminishing intermit-

[1] Warner, "American Charities," rev. ed., 1908, pp. 50–53.

tency in service, inefficiency in work, and the alienation and dehumanization of the employed.

Social action fails to be comprehensive, sane, and patient until it recognizes this conservation of social energy. A zealous philanthropist applies himself, for instance, to the cure of the drink-habit, and it may at first appear to him as a specific and isolated evil, for which definite remedies, such as a pledge of abstinence or a law of prohibition, may suffice. The principle of correlation, however, soon discloses within the single problem of drink further questions of the home, the industrial order, and the human craving for pleasure, which must be met in any effective attack. What is this thirst which drives men to the saloon? It is by no means the thirst for liquor alone, but often a more compelling thirst for companionship and society. The saloon is the poor man's club, the only available substitute for a cheerful home, and the patronage of the saloon is in no small degree the consequence of the squalor of domestic life. Few men would find themselves untempted by the warmth and companionship of the bar if they had no alternative but the tenement or the street. Indeed, the drink-habit itself, in a much larger degree than many reformers have realized, is a consequence of bad food and of bad air; and temperance reform is likely to remain provincial and temporary if it does not correlate with its own activity the further demand for better homes, healthful pleasures, wholesome cooking, and resources for play.

The same correlation of the social questions appears in the larger schemes of social regeneration which, as never before, press upon the attention of serious minds. Nothing, for example, is more conspicuous in the literature of scientific socialism than the candid association of the problem of revolution with the problem of the family. The new economic order, it is frankly taught, involves a new domestic relation. The Woman Question and the Labor Question are one. Woman, in the new social order, teaches the most conspicuous of German Social-Democrats, "is to be both socially and industrially absolutely independent.... She is to be subjected to no semblance of ownership or exploitation; but to stand over against man free and equal, the mistress of her fate."[1] The transformation of industry cannot be contemplated, therefore, without recognizing the grave probability of a corresponding transformation in the nature of domestic life. Will the freedom of woman to acquire economic equality create a family group of a flexible and temporary character? Will the children of a family be transferred from the "exclusiveness" of domestic life to the paternal care of the State, so that we shall have "complete freedom in the sex-relationship; ... and ... state interference ... in the matter of child-bearing"?[2] Will the satisfaction of the sexual instinct be "pre-

[1] Bebel, "Die Frau und der Sozialismus," 10te Aufl., 1891, s 337.
[2] Pearson, "The Ethic of Freethought, 1888, p. 445.

cisely as much an individual and personal matter as the satisfaction of any other natural instinct"?[1] These are problems which, though they may appear remote from the question of economic redistribution, are in fact fundamental in the scheme of revolution; and it is by no means impossible that the acceptance or rejection of the socialist programme may finally be determined, not so much by its possible effect on the future of business and the distribution of profits, as by its possible effect on the future of the family and the distribution of children.

In a word, the more closely the various social questions are scrutinized, the more completely they disclose their interdependence. The student of social action, though he dedicate himself to a special task, finds himself inevitably involved in enterprises or questions with which he seemed to have nothing to do. There are many social problems, but one Social Question. There are diversities of operations, but one spirit. There are many social forces, but there is one social energy. The last word of social science — as of natural science — is the confession of the unity of the world. Here is the rational ground of courage in social action. Any stroke of service dealt at any point may have its effect in forms of social action which appear completely detached or remote. Disconnected and apparently fruitless efforts for social amelioration find their justification through

[1] Bebel, op. cit., s. 338.

the conservation of social energy. Each reform of the drink-habit accelerates economic progress; each movement for improved housing is a contribution to the integrity of the family; each provision of industrial justice postpones industrial revolution. "The law of the correlation of forces," remarks John Fiske, "which perhaps ought rather to be called the law of the transformation of motion, . . . affirms that whatever energy has been expended in doing work must reappear as energy."[1] That is precisely what occurs in social action. The momentum of one plan of service is transformed into the heat or light of another, and the energy expended reappears as energy in some new form of endeavor or hope.

Yet, though it be true that social science offers a practicable and inviting way of approach, it by no means follows that it provides an entrance to the Social Question. Even though it may lead one to the gate, it may leave one without a key. Two considerations seem to bring one to a halt as he follows this road. In the first place, the habit of mind developed by the scientific method, though applicable to the Social Question and even essential for its interpretation, does not precisely represent the motives and aims which the Social Question comprehends. The Social Question is not merely a collection of facts to be scientifically observed, but a human appeal for justice, pity, fraternity, or sacrifice, which must

[1] "Outlines of Cosmic Philosophy," 1875, I, p. 291.

be not only heard, but felt and obeyed. The habit of mind induced by the scientific method remains, on the other hand, neutral, tranquil, and unmoved, even in the presence of the most dramatic facts. The pathologist examines the changes of human tissue with equal concern for disease and for health, for bacteria which kill and for bacteria which cure. He is not the physician, concerned with the application of science to relief; his researches are an essential preliminary of the physician's work; but the physician supplements the scientific habit of mind with the practical aims of his vocation. It is the same with the approach to the Social Question. Social science is social pathology; but the Social Question waits for the healing touch of the social physician. Social science approaches a fort by the slow advance of trenches and parallels, but these operations of the engineers are but preliminary to the assault of the army in force. Social science lays a track on which the Social Question may move, but it does not provide the power which makes it move.

Two distinguished examples may illustrate both the necessity and the limitation of social science. Frédéric LePlay (1806-1882) was a French engineer of the highest standing, and in the course of his researches into the ores of various countries lived for considerable periods among wage-earners in different lands. There he applied the scientific habit of mind to the compiling of workingmen's budgets, recording with unprecedented thoroughness and precision the details of incomes and expenditures among peasants of the Ural Mountains, knife-grinders of London, French fishermen, Swiss watchmakers, and many other social types. LePlay's "Working People of Europe"[1] thus became a model of statistical method applied to social conditions, and a permanent organization of loyal disciples perpetuates his spirit and aim.[2] Charles Booth is an English merchant, concerned with large interests of trade, who has dedicated to social research the training and experience of a commercial career. The observation and analysis which LePlay devoted to various countries, Mr. Booth has concentrated upon the single problem of the people of London, and with infinite thoroughness and munificent generosity has accomplished the prodigious task of a social classification, covering the four million inhabitants of the metropolis.

Here are two achievements of social science which indicate the essential prerequisites of effective service. The Social Question of Europe was for the first time defined by LePlay; the Social Question of London was for the first time clarified by Charles Booth. It was as though the channels through which social navigation must steer were at last surveyed, so that those who sailed the troubled waters might have a chart in their hands. Yet

[1] "Les Ouvriers Européens," 1855, 2me ed., 6 vols., 1877–79.
[2] "*La Réforme sociale.*" Bulletin des Unions de la Paix Sociale, fondée par F. LePlay.

neither LePlay nor Booth was directly concerned with an answer to the Social Question. Neither of these great explorers was by profession a philanthropist or a reformer. The first brought to his inquiry the mind of an engineer, the second that of a man of business. LePlay investigated social types as he might have investigated a mine before advising its purchase. Charles Booth studied the problem of London as he would have studied a new market before venturing into the risks of trade. It was for others to utilize these conclusions in the practice of relief. The man of science had shown the way which the man of practice must go. With noble self-effacement Mr. Booth announces this self-limitation in the last words of his work: "The object of these sixteen volumes has been to describe London as it appeared in the last decade of the nineteenth century. . . . For the treatment of disease, it is first necessary to establish the facts as to its character, extent and symptoms. Perhaps the qualities of mind which enable a man to make this inquiry are the least of all likely to give him that elevation of soul, sympathetic insight, and sublime confidence which must go to the making of a great regenerating teacher. I have made no attempt to teach; at the most I have ventured on an appeal to those whose part it is. . . . The dry bones that lie scattered over the long valley that we have traversed together lie before my reader. May some great soul, master of a subtler and nobler alchemy than mine, disentangle the confused issues, reconcile the apparent contradictions in aim, melt and commingle the various influences for good into one divine uniformity of effort, and make these dry bones live, so that the streets of our Jerusalem may sing with joy."[1]

There is a second characteristic of social science which indicates its limitation as an approach to the Social Question. When the student of physical science has passed from observation to generalization, and from generalization to correlation, he is confronted by a further question which is still more comprehensive and fundamental. What, he now asks himself, is the nature of this unity which is revealed behind the multiplicity of facts? What is this Energy which is thus conserved in these correlated expressions? Before this final problem of the unity of the physical world the scientific mind is silent. Here is the region of the Unknowable, the mystery of the universe. Here, in Spencer's words, we "come once more to that ultimate truth in which, as we saw, Religion and Science coalesce. . . . Deeper than demonstration — deeper than definite cognition — deep as the very nature of mind, is the postulate at which we have arrived."[2] "Amid the mysteries which become the more mysterious the more they are thought about, there will remain the one abso-

[1] Booth, "Life and Labour of the People in London," 1903, XVII, pp. 215, 216.
[2] "First Principles," 1869, pp. 189, 192.

lute certainty, that he is ever in the presence of an Infinite and Eternal Energy, from which all things proceed."[1]

The student of social science applies this language to social facts. As there is a physical energy from which all things proceed, so there is a social energy which binds the scattered phenomena of society into unity and meaning, and makes them witnesses of social order and progress rather than of accident or chaos. When, however, one proposes to define this social energy from which all things proceed, he has reached the boundary of social science, and passes into the province of social metaphysics. "Science," John Fiske has said, "studies the parts, philosophy studies the whole. . . . The doctrine of the correlation of forces lies on the border-line between the field of science and the field of metaphysics. It belongs in the transcendental region of physical science."[2] It is the same with social science. Beyond the region where social facts may be collected and analyzed, even on the great scale of researches like those of LePlay and Booth, lies a transcendental region, inviting and perhaps irresistible to the speculative mind, where guesses at the nature of things and hypotheses concerning the unity of the social world tempt the venturesome inquirer. What is this region which lies beyond the limits of science, and within which the

[1] "Principles of Sociology," Amer. ed., 1897, III, p. 175.
[2] Op. cit., I, pp. 40, 290.

inner unity of social facts seems concealed? This is the region occupied by the philosophy of society which has received the title of sociology; and through this transcendental region a second, and a fascinating, road seems to approach the Social Question.

The word "Sociology" was, it is believed, invented — and was apologetically defended — by Comte. "I may venture," he says, "to propose this new phrase, precisely equivalent to the expression already employed by me, social physics. . . . The necessity for some such nomenclature will, I hope, excuse me for this final exercise of a legitimate right, . . . without failing to express a profound repugnance for the habitual use of systematic neologisms."[1] Sociology was thus to Comte the last of five fundamental sciences — astronomy, physics, chemistry, physiology, and social physics — and the final problem of the Positive Philosophy was that of the emancipation of sociology from its "theologico-metaphysical infancy, and the application to human society of the same natural laws which interpret combinations of chemical elements and the movements of the stars." Sociology therefore, as originally expounded, was a biological

---

[1] "Cours de philosophie positive," 1839, IV, p. 252, *note*. This repugnance to neologisms did not deter Comte from the alarming proposition that "The word Sociology has already been adopted by all Western thinkers from my Positive Philosophy. It may be hoped that the words Sociolatry and Sociocracy will soon become current also." "System of Positive Polity," tr. Bridges, 1875, I, p. 327, *note*.

science, according to which the structure of society rested on purely material foundations. "The subordination of social science to biology," Comte said, "is so evident that nobody denies it in statement, however it may be neglected in practice."[1] The time was soon to come, however, when this social biology was to be first questioned, and then generally discredited. It became increasingly difficult to force the complex facts of human life into the limits of physics, and the growth of a biological organism was soon seen to present no complete analogy with the growth of a socialized world. "The sense of obligation," as Stein has said, "can never be derived from biology."[2] A more effective key to the secret of the social order seemed offered by psychology; and it has opened the door to many suggestive hypotheses concerning human organization and experience. Thus it has happened that the history of sociology has been in large part made up of animated discussions concerning the character and place of the new science, or, as it has been lately called, "The vindication of sociology."[3]

Yet whatever have been the dissensions of the sociologists, as to their fundamental doctrine they have been substantially agreed. Sociology, it has been uniformly maintained, is the final science,

[1] "Positive Philosophy," tr. Harriet Martineau, 1858, p. 486.
[2] "Aus der Biologie lässt sich nie und nimmermehr ein Sollen ableiten," op. cit., s. 222.
[3] *American Journal of Sociology*, July, 1909, pp. 1, 96.

the comprehensive synthesis, the circle of truth of which all other truths about human life are segments. Comte himself expressed this sense of climax when he said, "There remains one science, to fill up the series of sciences of observation, — social physics."[1] The same consciousness of a high calling reappears in almost every teacher. Sociology, according to one American master, "is the comprehensive science of society, co-extensive with the entire field of the special social sciences. . . . Its far-reaching principles are the postulates of special sciences, and as such they coördinate the whole body of social generalizations and bind them together in a large scientific whole."[2] "Sociology," affirms another text-book, "is subsequent to all these sciences, and dependent upon them."[3] Sociology, according to Professor Ward, "is the cap-sheaf and crown of any true system of classification of the sciences, and it is also the last and highest landing on the great staircase of education."[4] It is "the ultimate science for the perfection of which all other sciences exist."[5]

If, however, sociology is all this, if it is subsequent to all other sciences and dependent on them, if it is the cap-sheaf and crown of the sciences, the

---

[1] "Positive Philosophy," tr. Martineau, 1858, p. 30.

[2] Giddings, "Principles of Sociology," 1896, p. 33.

[3] Small and Vincent, "Introduction to the Study of Society," 1894, p. 32.

[4] "Outlines of Sociology," 1904, p. 20.

[5] Ward, "Dynamic Sociology," 1883, I, p. 9.

highest landing on the staircase of education, must it not be regarded as beyond the reach of ordinary minds, and accessible to encyclopædic scholars only, like Spencer and Comte? Does sociology, thus defined, offer a practicable way of approach to the Social Question? In one sense, no doubt, every one who thinks about the Social Question is sociologizing, just as every one who thinks at all is philosophizing; but the more of supremacy and finality is claimed for sociology, the more elusive and intangible this vast synthesis becomes. "The word "sociology," it has been truly said, "will not be put by"; but, as the same author not less truly remarks, it appears to many minds to represent "a penumbral political economy, — a scientific outer darkness."[1] Sociology, in fact, seems in its present condition to occupy that transcendental region which is irresistibly inviting to speculative minds, but which one must enter with the understanding that he has passed beyond the boundary of verifiable truth. This new doctrine of society, remarks the most distinguished of German economists, "proposes to comprehend and interpret the total content of social phenomena. . . . Here is certainly a gigantic task, which one can hardly undertake until he has at least begun to have a scientific and specific knowledge of a series of special sciences, such as government, economics, finance, and statistics."[2] In a more frivolous vein the late Prime Minister of Great Britain, Mr. Balfour, has

---

[1] Giddings, op. cit., pp. 28, 29.   [2] Schmoller, op. cit., I, s. 72.

with characteristic audacity suggested that the sociologists are like promoters of a new watering-place, where the plans of streets are visible, but where there are as yet no permanent inhabitants. In spite, then, of many important contributions to the interpretation of society, sociology appears to be a science which is, at its best, still in the making, and where it is more legitimate to speak of a "sociological movement"[1] than of a sociology which has arrived. A province which is as yet so largely unexplored does not appear to offer a clearly defined approach to the Social Question. If the debates of the sociologists are still chiefly devoted to determining what society is, and what sociology is, it may not unreasonably be regarded as premature to find in sociology the key to society. If it be true that "the function of sociology is the mapping out of the whole scope of human experience," must not this vast adventure be postponed until the minor townships and coast-lines of human experience are more accurately surveyed?

One way of escape from an unmanageable sociology may be found, it is true, by an arbitrary shrinkage of definition, so that an organizer of boys' clubs, or a student of the drink-habit, may be loosely described as a sociologist, and the administration of poor-relief or immigration may be defined as "practical sociology." Another refuge from the difficulties of the situation has been found in the deliberate appropriation of the name for a

[1] Small, in *American Journal of Sociology*, July, 1909, p. 4.

special section of research, such as the study of primitive society. Under this usage the word sociology would follow the history of the word biology. A science of life coextensive with the entire fields of botany and zoölogy having proved an inconveniently comprehensive vocation, the title Biology has been arbitrarily restricted to the sciences which deal with the beginnings of life or its elementary forms. In the same way sociology may retreat from its universal sphere, and content itself with the provinces of social embryology and social morphology. Either, it would seem, one must accept for sociology an arbitrary *minimum* or else must commit himself to a speculative *maximum*, where there may be unlimited range for ingenuity and suggestiveness, but where the vastness of territory is bewildering to all but the most venturesome minds. Sociology then, with all its fascinations, is an approach to the Social Question which may easily promise more than is likely to be attained. One line of advance may seem tempting until it is crossed by an equally inviting path. The infinite complexity of the social order yields itself with difficulty to a single formula. Social science leads irresistibly toward sociology, as physical science leads irresistibly toward metaphysics; but both sociology and metaphysics are rather ends to reach than ways to go. Sociology, like dirigible ballooning, may easily become a passion for inventive minds, but it is still involved in great difficulties of balance and steering, and remains for the present very much in the air.

If, then, social science provides the method along which approach must be made, sociology appears to offer the ideal which that method may some day hope to realize. If the one is a way toward the Social Question, the other is the view which may be reached when the whole of human experience lies plainly before the mind. If social science leads one to a point where he sees, as it were, from afar the nature of the Social Question, sociology seems to await him at the point where the entire plan and structure of the Social Question are completely clear. The one may bring us to the gate of the Social Question, the other lies within its closely guarded walls. It was said of a distinguished English scholar that science was his *forte* and omniscience was his foible. The sociologist may recognize a similar peril in his calling. Social science he may hope to make his *forte*, but he may not unreasonably be on his guard against the foible of omniscience.

III

ECONOMICS AND THE SOCIAL QUESTION

WHEN one turns from the ways of social science and of sociology to the way of economics, the approach to the Social Question appears to become less obstructed and obscure. The facts with which the Social Question is concerned are for the most part economic facts. Work and idleness, city life and rural life, housing, drink, food, — these and many other economic conditions and problems meet one at the threshold of the Social Question. Is he not, therefore, entering the province of economics, and is not the student of economic principles on the straight road toward the interpretation of the Social Question? If social science has given him a method, and sociology an ideal, has he not in economic science a key which fits the lock and opens the gate of the Social Question?

This confident approach to the economic interpretation of social life is, however, soon arrested by the controversies of the economists themselves. Is political economy a pure, abstract, deductive science, depending, as has been said, "more on reasoning than observation;"[1] or is it an inductive science, based on history, statistics, and "the much more crude and uncertain, yet indispensable method — if it may be called a method — of daily observation and general experience"?[2] Is it indifferent to social welfare, or is it an instrument of social welfare? Is it a weapon in the hands of the capitalist for the suppression of the wage-earners, or may that weapon be wrested from the capitalist by an organized revolution? Is political economy to be regarded as an unmoral science, or an immoral science, or a moral science? Each of these views has had its advocates, and each view leads to a different conclusion concerning the relation of economics to the Social Question.

In the first place, economic science may offer itself as a sufficient interpreter and guide of social progress. Such was the inference once drawn from Adam Smith's gospel of industrial freedom as reduced to orthodox doctrine by Ricardo. If it be true that the individual in pursuing his own self-interest is at the same time contributing to the common good; if the free competition of individuals is the safest road to the general welfare; if, still further, the laws of social action are as unalterable as the laws of nature, so that, as De Quincey said, Ricardo "had deduced, *à priori*, from

---

[1] Senior, quoted by Keynes, "The Scope and Method of Political Economy," 3d ed. rev., 1904, p. 16.

[2] Wagner, "Jahrb. für Nat.-Oekonomie und Statistik," 1886, XLVI, s. 237.

the understanding itself, laws which first shot arrowy light into the dark chaos of materials, and had thus constructed what hitherto was but a collection of tentative discussions into a science of regular proportions, now first standing upon an eternal basis,"[1] then the less these laws are obstructed in their action by sentiment or by philanthropic enthusiasm, the more stable will be in the end the social order. "The obvious and simple system of natural liberty," as Adam Smith called it,[2] should be trusted with the work of social redemption. Economic principles neither can nor should be altered. They operate to produce an economic harmony which, as interpreted in the fervid French of Bastiat, manifests "great Providential laws" and exhibits, like religion, "Providential intention."[3] "*Laissez faire*," "*Laissez passer*" thus becomes the first maxim of social wisdom. "All legitimate interests are in harmony. . . . He who has arranged the material universe has not withheld his regard from the arrangements of the social world. . . . The invincible social tendency is a constant approximation of man towards a common moral, intellectual and physical level."[4]

This economic optimism, however, was the product of circumstances which are now everywhere

---

[1] De Quincey, "Confessions of an English Opium-Eater," Works, 4th ed., 1878, I, 255.

[2] Keynes, op. cit., p. 40.

[3] "Harmonies of Political Economy," tr. Stirling, 1880, pp. 40, 517.   [4] Bastiat, op. cit., pp. 33, 46.

outgrown. The historical method applied to economic facts soon undermined the conception of an abstract and absolute science; and the teachings of Adam Smith suggested the inductive method of Malthus not less legitimately than the deductive method of Ricardo.[1] More than all, the growth of the great industry, with its new forces of combination and new accumulations of wealth, made this easy faith in equality and liberty no longer possible. Instead of the free competition of equal industrial units, the new economic world exhibited a vast inequality in opportunity and an enormous aggregation of industrial units. It was, in fact, an industrial revolution, in which, as Arnold Toynbee said, "The bitter argument between economists and human beings has ended in the conversion of the economists."[2]

The transition may be illustrated by the contents of a forcible and witty treatise, in which an American economist, as late as 1883, applied the principle of *Laissez faire* directly to the treatment of the Social Question. Under the title: "What Social Classes owe to Each Other,"[3] Professor Sumner frankly announced: "We all owe to each other good-will, mutual respect, and mutual guarantees of liberty and security. Beyond this nothing can be affirmed as a duty of one group to another in a

[1] Cf. Keynes, op. cit., p. 11 ff.
[2] "Lectures on the Industrial Revolution," 1887, p. 1.
[3] Sumner, "What Social Classes owe to Each Other," 1883, pp. 39, 169.

free State. . . . A free man in a free democracy has no duty whatever toward other men of the same rank and standing, except respect, courtesy, and good-will." This protest against the tendencies and maxims of much philanthropy and legislation was not without justification. It was provoked by the busy-bodies and sentimentalists of modern life, "the social meddlers" who interfere with economic laws, the "social doctors" who are ready with panaceas for the relief of the world. The mischief perpetrated by these persons was expressed in an amusing formula. Let A and B represent the social doctors, and D represent the person whom they propose to help — the pauper, the unemployed, or the criminal. How, then, do A and B proceed to help D? Do they help him themselves? On the contrary, they proceed to organize a society and enlist others to help him. If C, then, represents the people who are in fact helping D, then the formula will read: A and B get C to help D. The philanthropists, that is to say, exploit the sympathy of the self-supporting for the relief of the worthless. And who is C? He is the "forgotten man," the victim of A and B in their philanthropic zeal. No one wastes any sympathy on C. He is not a social problem. He is simply earning his honest living, and his earnings go to help D, who earns nothing.

All this, as an argument against impertinent philanthropy, or what Professor Jevons once called, "grandmotherly legislation," is as convincing as it is witty. The author, however, proceeds to translate this risk of social service into a general law. Wherever, he teaches, the amelioration of D is made at the cost of C, it is an interference with the natural course of economic distribution, and therefore in the end is certain to do harm. To lift one person up another must be pushed down; and the lever by which D is lifted rests on C, the forgotten man. When, therefore, one gives alms to the worthless, he takes wages from the worthy. When he gives work to the tramp, he takes work from the workingman. What, then, do social classes owe to each other? They owe nothing to each other. The "one big duty" is to take care of oneself. Here we are, "back at the old economic doctrine: *laissez faire*, let alone, mind your own business." To take from C and give to D is "to waste capital and overthrow civilization." The social world, like the physical world, must be taken as it is, and to intervene among its processes is to court disaster. The laws of industry, like those of nature, may work hardly, but in the end work justly; and the only sound rule of conduct is that of conformity and adaptation to these laws. Economics, as the same author has lately said, "has been almost robbed of the character of a serious discipline by converting its discussions into ethical disquisitions."[1]

This application of the earlier economics to the Social Question is so unlike the teaching which is

---

[1] Sumner, "Folkways," 1907, p. 37.

familiar to modern ears that it has an effect of
novelty as well as of audacity, and it measures the
distance which public opinion has traversed within
a single generation. For suppose that one finds
himself in the position of D, the man that is down;
or suppose that C, the forgotten man, is touched
by the modern sense of fellowship and responsibility, so that he "feels the suffering of the masses
as a burning pain,"[1] how is he likely to be impressed
by this pleasant doctrine of social salvation by
economic laws? May he not be provoked to passionate protest against a science which promised
so much and fulfils so little? If the workingman
believes that political economy is against him, may
he not conclude that the workingman should be
against political economy? If the inequalities and
inequities of the social order are to have no other
way of relief than the tardy operation of economic
laws, what can be anticipated but a reckless *dictum*
like that of Proudhon: "Political economy, which is
regarded by many as the philosophy of wealth, is
in fact nothing but the organized practice of robbery
and misery. . . . Political economy and law form,
according to socialism, the complete theory of iniquity and discord?"[2] A labor agitator in Boston
announced the same view when he said: "Economics is the weapon of the capitalistic classes; it
is the science which says to the workingman,
'Abandon hope!'" The more confidently, that

---

[1] Stein, op. cit., s. 418, and *note*.
[2] "Système des Contradictions économiques," 1872, I, p. 38.

is to say, the doctrine of economic harmony is pressed, the more abruptly it reacts into the doctrine of revolution. Ricardo, as Arnold Toynbee said, was the parent of socialism. If the only safe principle of economics be to mind one's own business, if social classes owe each other nothing, then the teaching, which thus fails to interpret the new social spirit, is likely to forfeit its primacy and to become the provocation of a new teaching of reaction or despair.

Such was, in fact, the curious course of history which led from the decline of *Laissez faire* to the rise of "scientific" socialism. Nothing at first sight could seem more remote from each other than the earlier optimism and the succeeding revolt; yet both Lassalle and Marx regarded their doctrines as the logical development of orthodox economics. According to Lassalle the iron law of wages was inexorable in its effect within the system of private property. "Wage-earners and wages constantly fluctuate about the line which represents at any period the minimum of necessities for existence. Sometimes wages and wage-earners are slightly above, sometimes slightly below that line; but the line never changes."[1] Marx also indicates the unconscious preparation for his work in the earlier political economy. "Its last great representative, Ricardo," he says, "in the end consciously makes the antagonism of class interests, of wages and profits, of profits and rent, the

[1] "Offenes Antwortschreiben," 5te Aufl. (date not given), s. 15.

starting-point of his investigations, naïvely taking this antagonism for a social law of Nature. But by this start, the science of bourgeois economy had reached the limits beyond which it could not pass." Marx further alludes to the "excellent work" of a Russian economist who had "referred to my theory of value, of money and of capital, as in its fundamentals a necessary sequel to the teaching of Smith and Ricardo."[1] But what was the inference drawn by these new teachers from the supremacy of economic law? Was it the inference of acquiescence and resignation? On the contrary, it was that of revolution. If economic laws under present conditions condemn the wage-earner to dependence, if each lift to D involves a harm to C, if social classes are set asunder by natural laws, if the labor which was the original source of value is through the operation of these laws confiscated by capital, then the social order itself, in which such inequity is inevitable, carries in its own nature the prophecy of its disruption, and the economic theory which justifies such wrongs must share the fate of the social institutions which it explains. The revolt against *Laissez faire* was not, therefore, as it has sometimes appeared to be, a revolt against economics. On the contrary, the new social order was to be interpreted by a new economics; and this new doctrine proved to be quite as rigid as the teaching which it was designed to supplant.

[1] "Capital," tr. Aveling, Pref. to 2d ed., pp. xiv, xv; cf. also p. 33.

Marx had the misfortune to be bred in the neo-Hegelian materialism of his time, and applying this materialism to his new gospel of human brotherhood and unity set as its foundation the dogma of "economic determinism." "The mode of production in material life," he taught, "determines the general character of the social, political, and spiritual processes of life. It is not the consciousness of men that determines their existence, but, on the contrary, their social existence determines their consciousness."[1] Here, as Engels wrote, was "the fundamental proposition which . . . belongs to Marx." "In every historical epoch, the prevailing mode of economic production and exchange, and the social organization necessarily following from it, form the basis upon which is built up, and from which alone can be explained, the political and intellectual history of that epoch."[2] The doctrine has had profound effect in shaping the philosophy of revolution. It gives simplicity and directness to action, and regards all other schemes of social amelioration as superfluous obstructions of the supreme end of economic change. "The thorough-going expropriation of all instruments of production makes the new foundation of society. Conditions of life and work for both sexes — manufacture, agriculture, commerce, education, mar-

[1] "A Contribution to the Critique of Political Economy," tr. Stone, 1904, p. 11.
[2] Marx and Engels, "Manifesto of the Communist Party," Engl. tr., 2d ed., 1898, p. 7.

riage, science, art, social life — in a word, the whole of human existence will then be transformed."[1] Popular instruction has disseminated the same doctrine in coarser forms. "Out of this unjust and unholy condition of things," a Socialist Catechism is reported as teaching, "nearly all the social evils and errors which afflict mankind have arisen, — war, hatred, jealousy, revenge, covetousness, greed, theft, usury, betting, lying, drunkenness, crime, and diseases of every kind — yes, and death itself."[2]

This original faith in economic determinism, however, which Engels described as the crowning glory of Marx, was soon confronted by the same difficulties which every philosophy of materialism has to meet. The very simplicity of its formula made it incapable of interpreting the complexity of modern life. The "form of production" does indeed gravely affect the progress and prospects of the wage-earning class, but it is not less evident that there are many other influences besides the form of production which stimulate or repress their desires and aims. Education, organization, class-consciousness, the sense of wrong, the demand for justice, — these, and a hundred other extra-economic motives, enormously complicate the Labor Question. Conditions, it is quite true, often determine consciousness, but quite as often con-

---

[1] Bebel, op. cit., s. 261.

[2] "Socialist Ten Commandments," issued by the Glasgow Socialist Sunday School Union, cited by the *London Times*, January 22, 1909.

sciousness determines its conditions, and, as Chalmers said, character becomes the parent of comfort. Many lives, it must be sadly confessed, have become the slaves of the machine, with their human hopes brutally determined by their economic fate. The child of the tenement lags in the race of life; the factory-hand loses the capacity for adjustment to new ways of work; to him that hath is given, and from him that hath not is taken even that which he hath. Philanthropy and religion concur with the teaching of revolution in demanding the rescue of human lives from the circumstances and inheritances which crush and enslave them. But to commit the entire social order to this economic fatalism is to take slight account of the capacity for self-recovery and self-discovery which illuminates the story of human progress, the emergence of self-respect out of squalor, and self-help out of helplessness, and thrift out of destitution, which is the hope of all philanthropy and the test of all economic wisdom. "Character," Mr. Lewes said many years ago,[1] "is to outward circumstances what the organism is to the outward world, living in it, but not determined by it. . . . Various characters live under identical circumstances, excited by them, not formed by them. . . . Character builds an existence out of circumstances; our strength is measured by our plastic power." In short, the earlier orthodoxy of socialism — though the polar opposite of the orthodoxy of *Laissez faire*

[1] "Life and Works of Goethe," 1856, I, p. 29.

— accepted the same way of redemption and erred by the same defect. Both faiths were attempts to reduce to terms of economics a phenomenon much too complex for so simple a formula. *Laissez faire* maintained that the social order left to its economic laws would issue into peace; socialism maintained, not less rigorously, that the inevitable issue of these laws was revolution; but both were alike in teaching that the social problem was an economic problem, when in fact both were standing at the threshold of a new world which neither economic liberty nor economic determinism could interpret or control. Marx, as Stein has said, " was rash enough to risk his entire social philosophy on the fate of materialism as a philosophical interpretation of the world. With the victory or defeat of materialism stands or falls the proud structure of his sociological argument, and therein he has built upon the sand." [1]

The situation is the more serious for the socialist faith because it has been from the beginning much more than an economic scheme, and has won its way, not so much by the invincible strength of its economic principles, as by its poignant appeal to the motives of fraternity, justice, and hope. The signs of the times which have provoked the socialist revolt, — the excesses of luxury and want, the cry of the workers and the silence of the rulers — these are not so much signs of economic determinism as of human determination, not so much the evidences of a new science as the witnesses of a new senti-

[1] Op. cit., s. 400.

ment. In short, the economics of socialism have proved to many sympathizers more of a hindrance than a help in promoting the spirit of socialism. A great human movement of compassion and desire has found itself hampered by a philosophy of materialism, and has dragged along with it an economic interpretation of history which does scant justice to its real spirit and aim. Precisely as is the case with much religious orthodoxy, the dogma has come to be carried by force of emotion rather than the emotion stirred by force of dogma. It is not easy to promote a sacred cause with no better war-cry than a materialistic theory of history. Economic determinism is little better than *Laissez faire* as an appeal to action. Indeed, it may as logically lead to a passive quietism as to an aggressive campaign.

Whether the socialist movement can free itself from this historical tradition is as yet by no means clear, but it is evident that the need of such emancipation is felt. In commenting, for example, on the socialism of Mr. Lowes Dickinson, an American critic remarks with justice:[1] " To Mr. Dickinson socialism is no necessity of evolution, but the voluntary reaching of man toward the very highest ideal. . . . His acceptance of socialism is due to a condition of uneasy idealism. It is at bottom a religious question. . . . 'Where it [socialism] errs,' he says, 'is in the attempt to eliminate altogether the appeal of the ideal and to imagine the industrial forces themselves, indepen-

[1] *Atlantic Monthly*, June, 1900, p. 852.

dently of human choice, delivering from the womb of the class-war a babe of fraternity and peace.' There is only one thing to say of such a statement as this, that it is a flat contradiction of what, to an orthodox socialist, makes of his hope a scientific fact." Some of the most devoted of socialists have, however, gallantly faced this "flat contradiction," and have expressed their dissent from this rigid orthodoxy. "The materialistic theory," Mr. Spargo maintains, teaches "not that history is determined by economic forces only, but that in human evolution the chief factors are social factors, and that these factors in turn are *mainly* moulded by economic circumstances."[1] Still more explicitly the same heresy is confessed in later writings, which may well have shocked some orthodox believers: "The Socialist movement has outgrown the influence of the early Utopians, which touched even Marx and Engels. . . . Collective ownership is not the ultimate, fundamental condition of Socialism."[2] "The tide of crude materialism which was at its height in the late sixties and early seventies of the nineteenth century has receded. . . . It is obvious that we are in the presence of a new socialism of a quality and temper undreamed of by Marx and Engels."[3] It is the familiar story of a spiritual

---

[1] "Socialism," 1906, p. 76.

[2] *North American Review*, June, 1909, pp. 850, 849.

[3] *American Journal of Sociology*, July, 1909, p. 20. The issue is sharply joined in the *Hibbert Journal*, Jan., Apr., and July, 1909, and the protestant view thus summed up by Miss Scudder: "It is my steady contention that those of us who read history otherwise

heresy contending against the apparently overwhelming force of a historical creed; the spirit asserting itself against the letter, modernism against ecclesiasticism. It may be doubted whether this gallant protest can make any deep impression on the tradition of socialism. To the vast majority of believers the doctrine of Marx still carries the weight of a final authority, and the insurgents in Germany have been repeatedly confronted by a doctrine of infallibilism, and by an inherited pride in the "science" of socialism.[1] Yet it is not impossible that the destiny of the movement may be determined in this issue between an economic creed and a moral idealism. If the Marxian infallibilism is to dominate other countries, as it has thus far prevailed in Germany, its cardinal doctrine of economic determinism may share the fate of the "crude materialism" from which it sprang. If, on the other hand, it proves possible to idealize the socialist movement into a moral awakening of responsibility for the just distribution of the products of industry, it may exhibit "a quality and temper undreamed of by Marx" and more consistent with the modern conscience.

Economics, then, it may be concluded, however essential it is for social security, is not in it-

than the Marxians have an equal right in the socialist movement." *Hibbert Journal*, October, 1909, p. 192.

[1] Cf. Bernstein, "Die Voraussetzungen des Sozialismus," 12tes Taus., 1906; and the detailed discussion in Mazaryk, "Die phil. und soziol. Grundlagen des Marxismus," 1899.

self a sufficient instrument of social redemption. Neither the optimism of the earlier orthodoxy nor the fatalism of the earlier socialists has in it the note of humanity, sympathy, and responsibility which is heard in the Social Question. Does not this conclusion lead to an opposite alternative? Should not economic teaching consent to use a new language and annex to itself the region where these voices of the time are heard? In other words, should not economics, instead of being an unmoral science of commercial production and exchange, become a moral science, covering the province of human emotions and sympathies, and undertaking the new task of human redemption?

Such was the transformation of economics proposed a generation ago by Carlyle and Ruskin, and urged by both these great teachers with splendid eloquence and burning satire. "Cash payment," said Carlyle, "never was, or could except for a few years be, the union-bond of man to man. . . . If, at any time, a philosophy of *Laissez-faire*, . . . start up as the exponent of human relations, expect that it will soon end. . . . The Laws of *Laissez-faire* . . . will need to be remodelled and modified and rectified in a hundred and a hundred ways. . . . A man has other obligations laid on him, in God's Universe, than the payment of cash."[1] With the same apostolic fire Ruskin attacked the orthodox economics of his

[1] "Past and Present," III, Ch. 10.

time. It was, he said, like "a science of gymnastics which assumed that men had no skeletons. It might be shown, on that supposition, that it would be advantageous to roll the students up into pellets, flatten them into cakes, or stretch them into cables; and that when these results were effected, the reinsertion of the skeleton would be attended with various inconveniences to their constitution. The reasoning might be admirable, the conclusions true, and the science deficient only in applicability. Modern political economy stands on a precisely similar basis. . . . I do not deny the truth of this theory: I simply deny its applicability to the present phase of the world."

Over against this vain and illusory science Ruskin sets his doctrine of the spiritual nature of wealth: "A strange political economy; the only one, nevertheless, that ever was or can be: all political economy founded on self-interest being but the fulfilment of that which once brought schism into the Policy of angels, and ruin into the Economy of Heaven. . . . Political economy . . . consists simply in the production, preservation, and distribution . . . of useful or pleasurable things. . . . It teaches nations to desire and labor for the things that lead to life; and . . . to scorn and destroy the things that lead to destruction. . . . That country is the richest which nourishes the greatest number of noble and happy human beings. . . . *There is no Wealth but Life.* Life, including all its powers of love, of joy, and of admiration. . . .

The persons themselves *are* the wealth. . . . The true veins of wealth are purple, . . . the producing as many as possible full-breathed, bright-eyed, and happy-hearted human creatures. . . . Among national manufactures, that of Souls of a good quality may not at last turn out a quite leadingly lucrative one."[1]

It was a conversion of political economy which was like the conversion of a sinner, from the pursuit of self-interest to the law of love. The earlier economics as a body of doctrine was to die like a physical body and to rise again in the spirit of social service. Political economy was translated into ethics. The conscience of England was to control its economic life. When, however, Carlyle and Ruskin descend from these heights of prophetic denunciation and become the law-givers of a new economic world, it is evident that neither of them is equipped for this technical and prosaic task. Carlyle was essentially a moralist; Ruskin was primarily an artist. The first arraigned the social order for its lack of character, the second for its lack of beauty; and these passionate indictments still convict the Mammonism and materialism of modern life. When, however, these prophets proceed from criticism to creation, and in their turn undertake to construct an economic system to which modern business shall conform, the results are almost childlike in their insufficiency. Carlyle counsels a frank retreat from the conflicts

[1] "Unto this Last," Essays 1, 2, and 4.

of modern industry to the peace of mediævalism, where, as in an ancient monastery, the servants obey and the abbot rules. Democracy, Parliament poor-relief, liberty, none of these have saving power; still less that "brutish, godforgetting Profit-and-Loss Philosophy . . . which we hear jangled on all hands of us, in senate-houses, spouting-clubs, leading-articles, pulpits, and platforms."[1] Strong men, captains of industry, an aristocracy of talent, permanent obedience by the masses of workers, a just despotism, as on a man-of-war, — in these alone is to be found the hope of the Present, as there once was the security of the Past.

Ruskin proceeds less defiantly with his constructive plan. Brutal and vain as "mercantile economics" may be, he is aware that a scheme of exchange must be devised for a real world, and this scheme of exchange he derives, not from any principle of commercial supply and demand, but from the supply and demand of that true wealth which is life itself. If life itself be a test of value, if to be valuable is "to avail" or contribute to life, then a just exchange of value must be made in terms of life, man for man, and time for time, and the science of economics must apply itself to the promotion and enrichment of life. "I want a horseshoe for my horse. Twenty smiths, or twenty thousand smiths, may be ready to forge it; their number does not in one atom's weight affect the

---

[1] "Past and Present," III, Ch. 10.

question of the equitable payment of the one who *does* forge it. It costs him a quarter of an hour of his life, and so much skill and strength of arm to make that horseshoe for me. Then at some future time I am bound in equity to give a quarter of an hour, and some minutes more, of my life (or of some other person's at my disposal), and also so much strength of arm and skill, and a little more, in making or doing what the smith may have need of."[1]

Here, then, are great teachings of moral idealism which can never lose their impressiveness, even to those whom Carlyle calls: "the Modern Guides of Nations, Journalists, Political Economists, . . . or any two-legged animal without feathers." When, however, these teachings are seriously considered as economic programmes, devised to control the tides of industry, they are like forts of sand built by children on the shore. To abandon the modern movement of Democracy and revert to a feudal aristocracy is as vain a dream in industry as in politics; to base commercial exchange on the principle of human equality is to be confronted by the essential inequality of capacity or service, which made Ruskin's quarter of an hour more valuable than the blacksmith's. Carlyle's panacea is in the authority of the one and the subordination of the many; Ruskin's equally illusory faith is in the opposite belief that the one can be reduced to the level of the many. The one

[1] Op. cit., Essay 3.

teaching is that of social reversion, the other that of social revolution. Carlyle's aristocracy of talent was the prototype of Nietzsche's superman, "the final flower and ultimate expression of the earth"; Ruskin's theory of exchange was soon to be preached as a gospel of revolution, and utilized as a contribution to a movement in which he had neither faith nor hope.

More instructive, however, than the practical insufficiency of these social prophecies is their demonstration of the necessity for some form of economic science behind all schemes of social reform. Scorn as they might the prevailing economics of their time, neither Carlyle nor Ruskin could restrain himself from supplementing his moral prophecy by a new economics; and in each case, as might have been anticipated, the attempt was fruitless. The conversion of economics into ethics was, as often happens with the conversion of the heathen to Christianity, a loss of primitive virtues without the gain of a more substantial faith. Carlyle and Ruskin concur in testifying that a social scheme without an economic method is incapable of realization, yet neither of these masters of literature provides an economic method which is applicable to the modern world. Economic theory may in itself offer no social salvation, but neither righteous scorn nor æsthetic sympathy can accomplish that social salvation unless economic theory be substantial and secure.

If, then, it may be concluded that economic

science, even though not sufficient for social redemption, is essential to social efficiency, how shall its place in the approach to the Social Question be defined? The answer seems to be found in the distinction, illustrated in every form of research, between a pure science and an applied science. It is a distinction which cannot be at all points rigidly maintained. The same person may be concerned both with pure science and with its application. Thus a great master of pure economic science, John Stuart Mill, entitled his work: "The principles of political economy, with some of their applications to social philosophy." Yet, in the main, the difference in habit of mind and method of approach not only permits a distinction between pure and applied science, but makes it one which, as has been wisely said, has "scientific expediency." "Our work will be done more thoroughly and our practical conclusions will be more trustworthy, when we are content to do one thing at a time."[1]

It has proved, that is to say, of practical advantage to discriminate the sphere of general reasoning from that of applied maxims, and to detach the study of principles from the study of effects. Pure mathematics, for example, examines the relation of forms and numbers without concern for their existence as facts. It may assume that the sum of the angles of a triangle is equal to two right angles, or it may assume that sum to be less or more, and on either assumption may construct

[1] Keynes, op. cit., p. 47.

a geometry. Pure mathematics is none the less the essential prerequisite of the applied arts of construction, and the artisan or bridge-builder utilizes for his purpose the formula which the mathematician has proved. In the same manner pure chemistry analyzes the materials submitted to it, without reference to their effects as poisons or as antidotes, while the practising physician applies these results to his healing art. The same scientific expediency suggests that economics may be defined as a pure science, which is the essential antecedent of judicious service or relief. It is a difference not so much of intellectual fields, as of intellectual tempers. The same facts lie before the economist and the social reformer, but to the one they are materials to analyze, while to the other they are instruments to use. Poverty, crime, wages, unemployment, — these, which to the economist are subjects to be weighed and compared, are to the philanthropist calls to service and cries for help.

Yet this change in intellectual attitude does not lessen the value of economic theory. Before the cry for help can be answered the nature of the need must be understood. Pure science directs and sustains applied science. The bridge-builder who is to span the chasm between social classes, the physician who is to heal social diseases, must have his training in the mathematics or the chemistry of social life. "The characteristic feature of political economy," remarks the biographer of Adam Smith, "is abstraction from all but a particular kind of motive, for example, self-interest, and the deduction of conclusions from the hypothetical premises so found. . . . There is no department of exact knowledge which has not been built up by much the same method. Physical science deals with only one kind of the relationships of things. Anatomy, and even physiology, treat the interdependence of the parts of the organism as if that interdependence were of a mechanical character, and leave out of account what stares the observer in the face in daily life, that these parts derive their distinguishing significance from this, that they are the parts of a whole which controls them in a non-mechanical fashion."[1] The same warning against the neglect of pure science by zealous practitioners is uttered by Bacon in an often quoted passage. "Hence," he says, "like *Atalanta*, they leave the course to pick up the golden apple, interrupting their speed, and giving up the victory. But in the true course of Experiment, and in extending it to new effects, we should imitate the Divine Foresight and Order. For *God*, on the first day, only Created Light, and assigned a whole day to that work, without creating any material substance thereon. In like manner, we must first, by every kind of Experiment, elicit the discovery of Causes and true Axioms, and seek for Experiments which may afford light rather than profit. Axioms, when rightly investigated

[1] Haldane, "Life of Adam Smith," 1887, p. 150.

and established, prepare us not for a limited but abundant Practice, and bring in their train whole troops of Effects."[1] It is a teaching which many a precipitate philanthropist and reformer may well take to heart. To give one day out of seven to the creation of light may appear to delay unreasonably the Genesis of the better world, but it may well prove true that light is the first essential in any earthly Paradise, and that from causes and axioms investigated and established there may follow whole troops of effects.

Within the general area of the Social Question there is, then, a field for economic science, and at the same time a further region which lies beyond economics; and as one approaches the Social Question he passes, as it were, through the country where the language is that of economics and enters into another country with a new language of human passion and desire. What is this region which lies nearer to the centre of the Social Question, and what are the laws to which this interior region must conform? The answer to this question must already have become plain. The Social Question is a moral question. As one passes its gateway he hears the language, not of economic science, but of moral emotion, compassion, pity, or hope. As one observes its movements he finds them utilizing the machinery of economics, but supplying that machinery with, what Ruskin called its proper fuel, the motive-power of justice, sacri-

---

[1] "Novum Organum," ed. 1850, pp. 42, 43.

fice, indignation, loyalty, or love. In the course of Henry George's famous discussion of "Progress and Poverty," he remarks: "Our previous conclusions, irresistible in themselves, thus stand approved by the highest and final test. Translated from terms of political economy into terms of ethics, they show a wrong as the source of the evils which increase as material progress goes on."[1] It is precisely this translation from the language of economics into the language of ethics which to the plain mind first discloses the meaning of the Social Question. Behind the evils which economics considers stands the sense of wrong, and beyond the road to the Social Question which the economists follow lies the way of the social conscience. Industrial life may, in short, be regarded, as a great German economist has said, "either as a system of natural forces or as a system of ethical forces. It is each according to the point of view from which it is studied. . . . On its technical side it is unmoral, but in its connection with spiritual and social forces it is ethical."[2]

Each incident of the Social Question has this twofold character: its outward form and its interior spirit, its mechanism and its motive-power, its economics and its ethics; and until the student penetrates through the first of these aspects to the second, he may altogether fail to understand what is really going on. A strike, for example, is in its

[1] "Progress and Poverty," 1888, p. 305.
[2] Schmoller, op. cit., I, s. 59, 60.

form an economic incident. It is concerned with outward adjustments of wages or hours, and it may even happen that neither party to the conflict sees in it anything but an economic war. It seems to be provoked by economic conditions, and it must be fought out with economic weapons. When, however, one considers what are the resources on which each fighting force depends, what degree of persistence and tenacity is probable, and what sacrifices are likely to be endured, he becomes aware that all these conditions of success depend on the amount of moral protest or passion that can be enlisted, and the assurance that a wrong is to be righted or a right confirmed. Public opinion reënforces one or the other side; the sense of a grievance stiffens resistance; the demand for liberty makes a rallying cry. Without some such passionate conviction, either justifiably felt, or — as sometimes happens — unjustifiably created, an economic issue is not, as a rule, capable of being magnified into a cause which deserves suffering and sacrifice. The battle-field is the field of economic production, but the battle-cry is the cry for justice, humanity, brotherhood, a living wage. The passionate loyalty which creates a fighting army out of a mob is not a product of economic science, but a flame kindled in the human heart. The case is, in short, one which has been fitly described by Felix Adler as a condition of "ethical distress." Industrial principles which were sufficient for a less complex world, fail to satisfy the new needs of the wage-earners, and as a consequence there is on every hand a searching of the heart, a unity of the spirit, a pledge of loyalty, a summons to fraternity, a new gospel of industrial progress.

Here is the reason why many employers find a strike on the part of their wage-earners so unintelligible or insane. Work is steady, contracts are kept, conditions seem prosperous; but, of a sudden, for some trivial grievance, and even against their own commercial interest, these unreasonable working-people stop work. Must they not be treated as stupid cattle, who do not even know the way to their own crib and kick against the goad? On the contrary, this revolt which, from the point of view of economics, is so indefensible, is the best of evidence that the real issue is not commercial, but ethical; that somehow — legitimately or fictitiously — there has been created a sense of wrong or a demand for rights, or a passionate sympathy, which may even defy self-interest and encourage self-sacrifice, and which is not likely to be silenced by economic arguments or proofs. What is to be thought, for instance, of a strike which is said to have occurred in San Francisco in 1906, not for an advance in wages, but against such an advance? The pay of certain electrical workers had, it is reported, been raised from five dollars to six dollars a day; but this change had been demanded and obtained without the authority of the Central Council of the trade, and without the notice required by its compact with the employer.

The main body of the employees, therefore, struck, to their own and their employer's loss, against the successful action of their own companions, who had failed of loyalty to the larger interests of their fellowship. Preposterous as such action may appear on economic grounds, it is an illustration of the motives which govern many industrial issues. The employer, in this case, might well have regarded a strike as impossible when the demand made had been granted and the wages given were higher than ever; but the Union — whether wisely or unwisely need not be determined — called out its men at an economic loss in the interest of a class-conscious discipline. What some of them had gained as wage-earners must, it was concluded, be forfeited for the higher aims of unity.

The incident illustrates a further characteristic of many such encounters, which is often perplexing. It frequently happens that they occur, not when they may be most reasonably anticipated, but when they seem improbable or impossible; not when economic conditions are at their worst, but when they are at their best; not on a falling market, but on a rising market. The economic condition of the wage-earners of the United States, for example, in spite of many reactions and interruptions, has, on the whole, vastly improved during the last generation, and the statistics of American wages have become the envy of the world. Between 1890 and 1903, according to the Federal Bureau of Labor, the average wages of the country advanced sixteen per cent, the hours of work per week decreased three per cent, the number of persons employed advanced thirty-two per cent, and the retail prices of food rose but eight per cent. If then, as agitators have often taught, the Social Question were essentially a stomach-question, if industrial peace were insured by an advance of wages double the advance in the price of food, then it would seem as if no further economic disturbance could visit the fortunate area of the United States. What does it mean, then, that under these prosperous circumstances industrial conflicts have become so determined, and the organization both of employers and employed has advanced on so vast a scale? It means that the motives which thus express themselves in economic forms must be sought, not in industrial conditions, but in ethical sensitiveness and desire. It is not so much a decrease in income which excites discontent, as an increase in intelligence and ambition. It is not that the wage-earners have less, but that they want more. "Let us assume," Professor Stein has said, "that the stomach-question is solved. Do you fancy that the Social Question is solved also? The gnawing stomach may be quieted, but the beating heart and anxious head are not content." The modern Labor Question, that is to say, is not, as is so often asserted, the sign of a social decadence, but rather the sign of a social renaissance. It meets a civilization, not on its way down, but on its way up. It is a witness, not of social degradation, but of social expectation. Its form is economic, but its motives are moral. It is the effort — often blind and groping, sometimes pitifully misdirected, — yet none the less proceeding from the conscience of the time — to shape economic life into an instrument of social justice and peace.

This interior character of the Social Question may be not less clearly seen if one turns from the evidence of industrial warfare to the methods proposed for industrial peace. A great variety of admirable schemes have been devised by benevolent employers for the convenience and comfort of their employed. Extra advantages, profit-sharing arrangements, provisions for housing, recreation, education, and sanitation — these, and many other plans of "welfare-work" have expressed the sense of paternal responsibility, and have converted many mercantile establishments into what the French have called an industrial family, — a "*famille ouvrière*." The conscience and the self-interest of employers concur in justifying such expenditure, and many a benevolent master surveys the scene of a well-housed, healthy, and permanent tenantry with a comfortable sense that his philanthropy does not decrease his dividends. What does it mean, then, that these generous and well-intended enterprises of welfare-work are so often met by suspicion and hostility, and that the provision of libraries, housing, baths, and playgrounds, which had appeared a guarantee of peace, have often become provocations to war? How monstrous such ingratitude appears to the benevolent employer, and how hopeless he may become of the future of the wage-earners, who so lightly reject his generosity and defeat their own ends! The cause of this scepticism is not, however, to be sought as the employer may fancy, in the stupidity of his employed, but on the contrary in their increasing intelligence and self-respect. They want as other people want, model homes and baths and concerts, but they want one thing else so much more that for it they will forfeit these economic gains. It is the right to live their own lives, to own their own homes, to choose their own amusements, and to spend their wages in their own way. At any cost they want liberty, and they will not accept as benevolence what they think they have earned as rights. They want to be employed, but they do not want to be patronized. In short, the reaction which is to be observed in all countries against the system of "welfare-work," or in its suggestive French title, of "*patronage*," is a further evidence that the Social Question cannot be answered in terms of economic advantage, but must take account at every step of the increasing alertness of mind and will in the wage-earning class. The employer who imagines that convenience and comfort are all that working-people desire is much more stupid than his employed. He fancies that he is dealing with an economic problem, when he has, in fact, before him a moral problem, — the problem of meeting the restless and sometimes volcanic activity of new desires, hopes, and dreams. Welfare-work was a solution of the Social Question when the wage-earners were an unawakened, toiling mass; but when the ideals of liberty and self-direction possess their minds, then comfort with patronage is likely to seem less desirable than the risks of freedom.

The Social Question is, then, an ethical question. Its branches stretch into every form of economic life, but its roots are in the soil of character, feeling, will, and hope. The approach to its interpretation must be surveyed by the engineers of economic theory, but must be travelled by the conscience of the modern world. This conclusion may seem to involve a new difficulty, created by the nature of ethical inquiry. Is not moral experience, it may be asked, naturally inclined to emotional and visionary methods, and is it not unfitted by its excitability and impressionability to be a judicious guide? Is not one confronted again by the precipitancy of the undisciplined conscience, and the evil wrought by good intentions?

This peril of emotion without direction, of heat without light, is obvious enough; but the possibilities of the ethical approach are illustrated in a striking manner by the history of economics itself. It is instructive to recall the fact that the three classical discussions which have had the most enduring influence on economic theory, are to be found in the writings of teachers who were not primarily economists, but who applied to economic problems the principles which they had already laid down in their ethical treatises.[1] The philosophy of Aristotle was the highest expression of the wisdom of Greece; the revival of Aristotle's teaching by Thomas Aquinas is still an authoritative statement of Catholic economics; and the "Wealth of Nations" of Adam Smith began the modern epoch in economic science. Yet not one of these masters approached the discussion of industrial questions as a professional economist. Each was primarily a philosopher, whose economic doctrine was a by-product of his general view of human life. Aristotle's theory of exchange was a corollary from his doctrine of Justice. "The object of our inquiry," he says, " is justice in the sense in which it is a part of virtue. . . . Of the Practical Justice and the Just involved in it, one species is that which is concerned with distributions of honor or wealth. . . . In dealings of exchange such a principle as this reciprocation forms the bond of union."[2] Thus, as a commentator on the "Politics" has remarked, "The end of political science is like that of all sciences, — the attainment of good, but good in its brightest form, the form of Justice."[3] The

---

[1] The fact is briefly noted by Ziegler, op. cit., 1891, s. 35; and, in the case of Adam Smith, dwelt upon by Jodl, "Volkswirtschaftslehre und Ethik" in v. Holtzendorff, "Zeit- und Streitfragen," XIV, Heft 224, s. 4.

[2] "Ethics," tr. Chase, Bk. V, Ch. III, VII, VIII.

[3] Lang, "The Politics of Aristotle," 1880, p. 5.

economics of Thomas Aquinas forms a section of his teaching on the principles of ethics.[1] He distinguishes between two forms of exchange, one using money for the necessities of life, the other exchanging money or commodities for the sake of gain. "The first form of exchange is praiseworthy, ... the second may be justly criticised in so far as it serves only the greed of gain." Finally, the "Wealth of Nations," though described by Pitt as the "best solution of the question connected with the history of commerce or with the systems of political economy,"[2] was the work of a professor of moral philosophy, and made the second part of a system, of which the first part was a "Theory of the Moral Sentiments." In concluding that treatise Adam Smith remarked: "The two useful parts of moral philosophy, therefore, are Ethics and Jurisprudence. . . . I shall in another discourse endeavor to give an account of the general principles of law and government. . . . I shall not, therefore, at present enter into any further detail concerning the history of jurisprudence;"[3] and in the preface to the eleventh edition, in 1808, he adds, "In the inquiry concerning the nature and cause of the wealth of nations I have happily executed this promise." Indeed, it would have much sur-

---

[1] "Die Summa Theologica des heiligen Thomas von Aquin," Regensburg, 1888, Bd. VII, "Die Sittenlehre"; especially Kap. 77, Art. 1-4, s. 471 ff.

[2] Haldane, op. cit., p. 75.

[3] 7th ed., 1792, II, pp. 394, 399.

prised Adam Smith to know that his first treatise would be forgotten, while the second would be remembered as the most important contribution of modern times to economic literature. "One ought not," says a contemporary, "perhaps to be very much surprised that the public does not do justice to the works of Adam Smith, since he did not do justice to them himself, but always considered his "Theory of the Moral Sentiments" as a much superior work to his "Wealth of Nations."[1] Historical precedents so notable as these, while they do not eliminate the risk of intemperate or misdirected leadership, may encourage those who find themselves led along the way of ethics towards the interpretation of the Social Question. The end of political science remains, as Aristotle taught, the attainment of good, and the discipline of the Moral Sentiments is, as Adam Smith recognized, preliminary to the securing of the Wealth of Nations.

The place of economic theory in the approach to the Social Question thus becomes plain. It may be indicated in the phrase which one of the greatest of modern philosophers uses to describe the principles of his own work. In the introduction to his "Mikrokosmus" Lotze announces the sublime thesis which his system is designed to represent: "It is to show," he says, "how absolutely universal is the extent, and at the same time

[1] "Life of Sir Samuel Romilly," 3d. ed., 1842, I, p. 308; a letter of August 20, 1780.

how completely subordinate is the part, which mechanism has to fulfil in the structure of the world."[1] Through the entire universe, from its material elements to its spiritual manifestations, according to the teaching of this master, work the invariable processes of mechanism, insuring the stability and continuity of the world; yet through this vast mechanism there is fulfilled a moral purpose, of which history and experience are the instruments and expressions. The same great proposition may be maintained concerning the modern social world. Its mechanism is that of the economic order, and on the precision and perfection of that mechanism the continuity of social progress depends. Yet this economic mechanism is the instrument of motives which it does not itself supply. Through the machinery of economic law works the power of the social conscience. Let that machinery be maladjusted, and progress becomes halting, intermittent, or precipitate; let the supply of motive-power fail and the machinery, however well constructed, becomes motionless and dead. Ethics without economics is like a railway train without brakes. It passes the point where it should stop, it pauses at the point which it should pass, and finally it exhausts its power and comes to a halt, not at its proper terminus, but in the woods. Economics without ethics, on the other hand, is like a train without steam, admirable in its equipment, but without the power which can move its wheels.

[1] 2te Aufl., 1869, s. xv.

Here are the two besetting faults of modern social service,— the trusting to a machine which has no power, and the trusting to a power which has no brakes. Who shall say whether more mistakes have thus been made by sentiment without science, or by science without sentiment? On the one hand is the peril of sentimentalism, on the other hand is the peril of officialism. On one side is the sin of soft-headedness, and on the other side is the sin of hard-heartedness. One of the wisest of American leaders in scientific charity enumerates as the four chief causes of pauperism: foul homes, intoxicating drink, neglect of child-life, and indiscriminate almsgiving.[1] Why is it that indiscriminate relief should be thus classified with slums, drink, and child labor as a cause of poverty? It is inspired by the most admirable emotions; it gives, hoping for nothing again. It may even pride itself on its uncalculating benevolence, as contrasted with the rigid methods of —

> "Organized charity, scrimped and iced,
> In the name of a cautious, statistical Christ."

Why, then, is indiscriminate almsgiving a sin? It is because it substitutes ethical emotion for economic law. It imagines itself to be in a world of feeling when in reality it is a world of facts. It proceeds as though the world were soft when in reality the world is hard. Sentiment without science in charity degrades the workless into the worthless,

[1] Paine, "Pauperism in Great Cities," 1893, p. 18.

and in relieving want breeds mendicancy. What it fancies to be benevolence is at bottom indolence. Its left hand does not know what its right hand is doing, but if it did know, it would be ashamed. On the other hand is the not less threatening peril which awaits a science of relief which is not an instrument of moral power. Officialism easily becomes mechanism; institutionalism tends to automatism. An agency of relief may become so wooden that it is fitly called a "Bureau"; and a human life may be dealt with so impersonally that it is properly called a "Case." How to rescue officialism from its own machinery and direct the mechanics of charity without losing faith or hope, — this is the difficult problem which makes the life of a professional agent of relief a constant struggle to save his own soul from the risks of his hazardous calling. It is easy to be recklessly kind, it is equally easy to be timidly wise; but to be scientifically sympathetic and prudently humane, — that is the complex task of modern philanthropy. What voluntary relief most needs is to be taught to think, and what official relief most needs is to be allowed to feel. In the vision of the Prophet Ezekiel there was seen a confusing complexity of wheels and of "wheels in the middle of wheels," but within the wheels there were living creatures and "when the wheels went, these went," for "the spirit of the living creatures was in the wheels."[1] It is a picture of social service under the

[1] Ezek. i. 29.

conditions of the modern world. Wheels there must be, and wheels within wheels, and the adjustment of this intricate mechanism is essential to effective philanthropy; but the wheels are moved by the power of love and the mechanism halts until the spirit of the living creatures is in the wheels.

The same story may be told of each social institution or undertaking. The family, for example, is in one aspect an economic fact. One of the pillars which support the family is the institution of private property. The family is the object of the man's earnings and of the woman's thrift. To neglect or despise the economics of the family is to court disaster. It is foolish sentimentalism to base the hope of domestic bliss on bread and cheese and kisses. The socialist teaching is justified in its insistence that a radical change in the economic order is likely to bring with it a radical change in the organization of the family. Common ownership of the instruments of production can hardly fail to affect "family exclusiveness," and to substitute the State for the family as the unit of society. Yet, on the other hand, to regard the family as wholly or as fundamentally an economic fact, as though it were a commercial arrangement or a piece of property to be bought or bartered, is to enter the highroad to domestic instability and disruption. Back of all the economic considerations which have consolidated the family lie the normal and permanent instincts of human love. The family is an ethical fact not less than an economic fact. It is the object of the sweetest sacrifices and the happiest self-forgetfulness. The family is the primer in the moral education of the race, and the issue which the present crisis in the history of the family represents is precisely the issue between the economic and the moral aspect of the family. Shall domestic life be regarded as a trade, or shall it be regarded as an ideal?

Even the industrial world, which seems so completely dominated by economic law, is not less demonstrably than the family or the work of philanthropy a moral fact. It rests on credit; it exists through integrity; it prospers through public confidence. Modern business, far from being, as it is often described, a pitiless system of piracy and plunder, is essentially a vast structure of social service, where economic gain, as a rule, coincides with public utility; and where, for one fortune procured by destructivism and fraud, a hundred are the consequences of integrity and fidelity. The best qualification for success in business is an endowment of sobriety, incorruptibility, hopefulness, and patience; and the more complex business has grown, the more dependent it has become at every point upon trustworthy character and incorruptible leadership. The economics of modern industry give a new significance to its ethics. Problems of new machinery are still difficult, but the most pressing problem of modern business life is to find new capacity to run the machinery which is already devised; and the power which creates this productive energy is to be sought — as men search among the hills for unused waterfalls — in the abundant, and as yet half-utilized, resources of moral initiative and strength.

Here, then, the approach to the Social Question draws nearer to its end. The mechanism of economics prepares the way for the advance of ethics. The wheels of the social order wait for the power of the social conscience. Up the highway, levelled and straightened by economic law, walks the student of the Social Question, until he reaches the main gate, and, listening there, hears within its walls the voices of moral passion and desire.

IV

ETHICS AND THE SOCIAL QUESTION

If the Social Question is in its interior nature an ethical question, if its incidents and movements, though in their form economic, are in their spirit and force the evidences of a social conscience, then the approach to the Social Question must be made along the way where the principles of ethics are the most trustworthy guides. The Social Question in this aspect is but the contemporary form which moral progress assumes, a chapter in the history of morals told in the language of the present age. Thus the relation of ethics to the Social Question becomes peculiarly instructive. The theory of ethics gives unity to the complex details of the Social Question, and the Social Question gives definiteness to the theory of ethics. What the history of ethics reports in the form of philosophy, the Social Question reproduces in the events of the modern world. What the theory of ethics dissects as dead material, the social conscience calls to life; and what is obscure in the Social Question is clarified when approached by the theory of ethics.

This reciprocity of action which associates ethics

with the Social Question has been, it must be admitted, much obscured by the traditional method of ethics itself. An abstract and speculative system, such as has often been expounded under the name of ethics, may have no intimate relation with the practical problems of the social conscience. A scientific analysis of virtues, vices, and passions may be as unlike the real emotions of a moral struggle as the subjects of a dissecting-table are unlike the human beings whose virtues, vices, and passions are silenced in death. It is important, therefore, to recall the nature of ethics, and to free it, first of all, from the appearance of remoteness and unreality which it has frequently presented.

Ethics, as its greatest masters have always taught, is as far as possible from the desiccated and arid science to which it has sometimes been reduced. It is, on the contrary, a science which deals with the most living of subjects,—life itself. Life, however, is not presented to the student as a fixed or finished fact. Life is a process, a growth, a developing, moving, self-propagating fact. It must be the same with the science of conduct. The study of life must be itself alive. It is not concerned with fixed alternatives of duty, but with character in the making, with motives in motion, with the evolution of right desires, with the education of the will, with the conversion of an untrained and intermittent sense of duty into that disciplined character which the Christian apostle calls a "good conscience." A consistent and final doctrine of ethics finds itself confronted by the fact that life itself is not consistent or complete, but rather a flowing stream of changing experience, like a river which is in its course one, but in its scenery forever new. At one moment the current of conduct struggles past the shoals of self-interest; at another moment it flows through tranquil reaches of idealism; yet through all these eddies and windings it is a continuous stream. One is never safely and irretrievably selfish, or wholly and consistently self-sacrificing. The same man may be an idealist when he is in love, and a materialist when he is hungry. The same man may fancy himself a confirmed sceptic or scoffer, only to be surprised by some sudden influx of enthusiasm or magnanimity: —

> "Just when we are safest, there's a sun-set touch,
> A fancy from a flower-bell, some one's death,
> A chorus-ending from Euripides, —
> And that's enough for fifty hopes and fears
> As old and new at once as nature's self,
> To rap and knock and enter in our soul,
> Take hands and dance there, a fantastic ring,
> Round the ancient idol, on his base again."

To study conduct therefore, as it is, is to study it in motion, as a series of imperfect adjustments, approaching a stable equilibrium. Morality is like bicycling; security is for those only who are moving, and disaster is for those who stop. "Forgetting those things that are behind, and reaching forward unto those things that are before," is the maxim of moral progress. This is what gives to the study of morality its perennial and dramatic interest. One never knows, in watching conduct, what demands and decisions may lie just beyond the next turn of experience. To read life truly one must run as he reads; to see life as it is one must see it on the wing. To study ethics is to follow the river of experience as it flows through light and shadow, among rocks and rapids, between the banks of time. "To describe myself as if I were a settled fact," one of the most beloved of American teachers has said, "is to make of myself a thing. My life is in that which may be. . . . Personality is an affair of degree. . . . We are chasing a flying goal."[1]

This primary trait of a vitalized ethics brings it into close relation with the nature of the Social Question, for here, also, one is concerned with facts not in rest, but in motion, with a world in process, with a stream of tendency, a broadening river of social obligation and agitation, which threatens disaster unless controlled, but which may be converted into a mighty power of efficiency and service. The Social Question, like the study of ethics, must take life as it is and watch the movement of the social conscience sweeping through the experience of the time, changeful and restless as a rapid stream, submerging standards which have seemed high and dry, and bearing upon its current the moral experiences of the modern world. A science of life thus ap-

[1] Palmer, "The Nature of Goodness," 1903, pp. 133, 140.

proached may not improbably offer a key to a living question. Ethics as a statical science may have little to report of this river of social duty; but ethics as a dynamical science may direct and control its flow, and transform its energy into social power. In a famous passage of the "Advancement of Learning" Bacon distinguishes between these two uses of "moral knowledge." "The main and primitive division of moral knowledge seemeth to be into the Exemplar or Platform of Good, and the Regiment or Culture of the Mind. . . . For the Nature of Good Positive or Simple, they [the ancient philosophers] have set it down excellently. . . . Notwithstanding, if before they had comen to the popular and received notions of virtue and vice, pleasure and pain, and the rest, they had stayed a little longer upon the inquiry concerning the roots of good and evil, and the strings of those roots, they had given, in my opinion, a great light to that which followed."[1] That is precisely the distinction which ethical philosophy must make before it approaches the Social Question. The Platform of Good has been set up by the philosophers quite above the turbulent issues of practical life, like stage scenery which the pit may admire yet knows to be unreal, but the ramifying roots of good and evil which spread through the soil of social life and create the Social Question, — these need a great light, which moral philosophy alone can give.

[1] "Works," ed. Spedding, London, 1857, III, pp. 419, 420.

There is a second characteristic of ethics which confirms this impression of a special adaptation to the Social Question. Ethics is itself a social question. Its roots lie in the soil of society, and its development proceeds through social adjustment and aims. It is true that ethics as a self-regarding and self-analyzing science has played a great part in the history of philosophy. Precisely as the "economic man" has been isolated by metaphysics and studied as the instrument of economic laws, so the "moral man" may be isolated by hypothesis and studied as the instrument of moral laws. As a matter of fact, however, neither of these men is more than a philosophical fiction. Conduct, whether economic or moral, is not isolated, but is inextricably involved with the give and take, the friction and momentum, of the multitudinous social life which the individual inevitably shares. Experience does not operate in a vacuum, but in the atmosphere of a social world. Life, to use the language of philosophy, is in relations; personality realizes itself in the social order. "So long as the single being exists in his own world, the idea of goodness does not begin. Only when various lives touch each other in their spheres of activity, phenomena occur to which we apply moral judgments. . . . All acts by which the sphere of another life is arbitrarily invaded are to be defined as bad. Acts, on the other hand, by which another existence is ameliorated are good; and the higher in moral estimate, the greater the sacrifice of one's own good."[1] "Intelligence and reason, conscience and language, emerge only through social, collective, or combined action. . . . This is in a nutshell the evolution of ethics. It begins where coöperative action appears upon the scene. . . . [Man] has gained a human soul, a social spirit. He has risen above himself, without leaving himself."[2]

The very words which ethics employs to convey its own teachings carry with it this implication of a social world. Thus the word "conduct" means guidance or leading, and only in its secondary sense is applied to personal behavior. In the same way the word "ethics" recalls the *ethos* or custom, through which conduct became fixed as habit or law. Duty is that which is due; obligation is the sense of being tied or bound. The fossil language of ethics thus reports the character of the rocks from which the science has been hewn. To speak of conduct, ethics, duty, obligation, is to affirm the social basis of morality. The Golden Rule, which has seemed, not only to Christians but not less to Confucians and Buddhists the perfect law of moral conduct, is a social maxim: "What you do not wish done to yourself, do not to others." "Do nothing to thy neighbor, which hereafter thou wouldst not have thy neighbor do to thee." "Whatsoever ye would that men should

[1] Ostwald, "Vorlesungen über Naturphilosophie," 1902, s. 450.
[2] Wallace, "Letters and Essays in Natural Theology and Ethics," 1898, pp. 122, 124, 129.

do to you, do ye also unto them." "History," concludes Stein, "knows no completely isolated individual. . . . As physics and chemistry study atoms not alone, but in molecules, so the science of sociology deals with socialized individuals. Though the naturalist may assume atoms to exist behind molecules . . . and the sociologist may assume the individual or social atom to exist behind the social group, . . . these assumptions are sheer abstractions, if not mere fiction."[1] "The moral drama," remarks one of the most brilliant of young American teachers, "opens only when interest meets interest, when the path of one unit of life is crossed by that of another. Every interest is compelled to recognize other interests, on the one hand as a part of its environment, and on the other hand as partners in the general enterprise of life. Thus there is evolved the moral idea. . . . Through morality a plurality of interests becomes an *economy*, or *community of interests*."[2]

If, then, ethics is essentially a social science, and if its problem is not merely the interpretation of personal conduct, but not less the direction of conduct in a social world; if character itself is a moving process of adjustment between one's own life and the life in common, then a second point of coincidence is found between the way of ethics and the way of the Social Question. The Social Question also, as has been already observed, pre-

---
[1] Stein, op. cit., 2te Aufl., 1903, s. 417, 418.
[2] Perry, "The Moral Economy," 1909, p. 13.

sents the same problem of the individual set in the social order, and determining his place in part therein. How to be a person within the sphere of the common good; how to develop the social groups of domestic or economic or political life without abandoning the rights or disturbing the growth of the individual; how to harmonize liberty with law, emancipation with organization, living growth with stable form, — this, which is the essence of the Social Question, is at the same time the problem of ethics. "Harmonize thy will with the world's will" is Royce's statement of the Moral Law. "Express thyself through obedience. Win thy victory by accepting thy task."[1] It needs but the slightest transposition of language to convert these phrases into a statement of the Social Question. "Harmonize thy will with the general will; express thyself through service; win thy victory by loyalty to the common good." The problems of ethics and of the Social Question, though different in form, utter the same desire for a better social world. Ethics looks for the character which shall control conditions; social service creates the conditions which may fortify character. The two streams flow in different channels and water different tracts, but their courses approach each other, until the river of ethics empties into the larger current of the Social Question, to deepen and purify it from the abundant sources of the history of human thought.

[1] "The World and the Individual," 1901, p. 348.

These similarities and affinities between ethics and the Social Question lead one, therefore, to recall in further detail the nature of ethics and its possible application to the problems of social life. What is this process which ethics traces as a principle, and which the Social Question exhibits as a fact? Can the story of ethics be freed from its technical and abstract language and studied in the simplest terms of familiar experience and conduct? The most elementary answer to this question may perhaps be reached if one turns for a moment from the teachings of the learned, and sets before himself the case of a single and normal life, as it passes from one to another phase of moral experience. One may begin, for instance, with a baby, as it enters the world of other people and finds the problem of social adjustment presented to its dawning mind. What is the normal attitude of the baby toward this world of other people? So far as one may venture to interpret the mystery of babyhood, the natural attitude of the baby toward the world is that of a splendid defiance. He asserts, as by Divine right, his absolute sovereignty. He "wants the earth" and expects to get it. If a conflict of interests arises between the world and the baby, so much the worse for the world. The baby wants the rattle, and with the same confidence wants the moon, and if either elude his grasp, he protests with tears. The social world to the baby is the nursery, with the nurse and adoring parents, and in this little world the baby is supreme.

His universe is a Ptolemaic system, in which all planets revolve about him as the central sun. The baby's ethics is thus an uncomplicated and delightful Egoism.

Soon, however, the social order takes its turn in self-assertion. The shades of the prison-house begin to close about the growing boy. His home, his parents, his teachers, assign him his part within the social whole. The plastic youth is shaped by the moulding world. His problem of self-discovery and self-development remains as commanding as ever, but the pressure of his social environment may no longer be ignored. His personal problem begins to take a new and a defensive form. Instead of defying the world, the youth adjusts himself to the world and establishes between it and himself an equation of rights. Here is his own life with its inalienable desires; but here also, on the other hand, is the not less inevitable compulsion of the life of others. Conciliation and arbitration begin to supplant untrammelled self-interest. The youth proceeds by compromise. He asks of the world all it can give; but its giving, he knows, must be equitable to all who ask. Thus the world of other people is set over against each person in an unstable equilibrium. What one gets, the other loses. The equation becomes difficult to maintain; the balance shifts; the adjustment is provisional, tentative, momentary. Here is the characteristic attitude of the changeful, impetuous, and disillusioned life of youth. There is a sudden appearance of worldly wisdom, a sanguine faith abruptly lost, the delicate balance toppling over into doubt or scorn. Character at this point is like a vessel which is touched by the first gust of rising wind, and feels itself swayed beyond its bearings until it slowly gathers headway and answer its helm.

Here, then, occurs, in the normal course of life, that critical transition which supplants the instability and breeziness of youth by the poise and momentum of moral maturity. Many lives, it must be confessed, fail to reach this new experience, and lie, like a motionless vessel, beyond the touch of a favoring wind; but few lives are so blind or careless that they do not see where the wind strikes or what it can do. Even when still becalmed in self-interest or expediency, they can at least watch other lives holding their course. Even though they may not themselves outgrow the babyhood or the youth of morals, they are aware that a riper experience lies beyond. What is the mark of this moral maturity, in which the quietness and stability of character are to be found? Curiously enough, it is attained only as one accepts as the law of life what has hitherto seemed impossible or absurd. To discover that to realize himself one must surrender himself, that to lose one's life is to save it, that loyalty is liberty, and service is freedom,—what could be more self-contradictory and paradoxical than this moral faith! Yet, precisely this moral paradox has throughout all human history opened the way to moral tranquillity, efficiency, and peace. Indeed, the paradox of morals is not more surprising or more impracticable than the paradox which meets one in all his experience in the world, and which at every point discloses the way of adjustment and power.

Such for instance, to cite the simplest illustration, is the summary of one's experience among the physical forces of the natural world. At their first approach they present themselves as alarming and threatening, and one may resist them as enemies or conciliate them as treacherous friends. As superstition ripens into science, and experience gathers authority, these forces of the physical world become, however, not obstacles to be encountered, but instruments of self-defence and power. A railway train is at each increase of its speed retarded by a corresponding increase of friction; or, to use the famous illustration of Kant, the dove "cleaving in free flight the air whose resistance she feels, may fancy that she might make her way with greater ease through airless space."[1] It soon appears, however, that the very conditions which seemed obstructive of motion are, in fact, the conditions on which all motion depends. Oil the track whose friction retards the train, and the wheels of the locomotive whirl round without propelling force. Set the dove under an exhausted receiver, and she lies perfectly free yet perfectly helpless, because

[1] "Kritik der reinen Vernunft," Einl., "Werke," ed. Hartenstein, 1868, III, s. 38.

no resisting atmosphere supports her wings. The swimmer wearily thrusts his arm against the opposing sea, but the resistance which compels his effort saves him from sinking. Physical security rests on this paradox of experience. We govern nature as we conform to her laws. Our service is our freedom.

The same paradox of experience meets one at every step in life. A business or profession, for example, offers at the outset little but drudgery and routine which must be tolerated or escaped, yet within these apparently restrictive conditions is hidden the secret of self-discovery and happiness. The rub of life gives to life its momentum. The way out of limitation is not round it, but through it. Strait is the gate and narrow the way which leads to life. It is the same with the life of learning. The self-limitation of the scholar is the self-discovery of the scholar. The smatterer, though he may know many things, misses the secret of the scholar. As the scholar commits himself to his special task a vista of learning opens beyond his narrow path, which could be seen from no other point, and along the way of the limited vocation the scholar walks with plodding steps toward the view beyond, until he finds himself, as Newton said, on the shore of an infinite ocean of truth, gathering a few shells from the beach of the unknown. It is the same, finally, with the experience of conduct. The environment of other lives is the atmosphere without whose resistance the individual cannot move. The same paradox, which interprets the physical and the intellectual life, is the key to ethics. Moral progress proceeds through social pressure. The friction of the social order sustains the wings of the will.

Here, for example, is the fallacy of the anarchist. He would abolish social pressure and escape from social restraint. He asks nothing of others and owes nothing to them. He is the consistent individualist. The social order is his enemy because it restricts his freedom. But is this freedom of the anarchist real? Is a country free when it is without law, or a man free when he is an outlaw? On the contrary, a lawless country may be the most oppressive of States. The freedom of a man is not like the freedom of a wolf, to ravage and rend; but rather the freedom to grow, to achieve one's best, to realize oneself, to expand the radius of efficiency, to enlarge the horizon of hope; and this expansion of aim is possible only within the social environment which appears to hamper and restrict. Social adjustment is the path to personal liberty. The function of the State is not to limit the individual, but to develop the individual. Liberty is not a defiance of law, but the perfect law is the law of liberty. Such is the natural issue of the processes of moral growth as it reaches moral maturity. The self-centred impulses are to be not discarded, but dedicated. The demand for rights is not denied, but answered. The moral paradox comes not to destroy but to fulfil. Fulness of life is breathed in the atmosphere of the common good. As babyhood is followed by youth, and youth ripens into manhood, so self-defence against the world and self-adjustment to the world prepare the way for self-discovery through service.

This story of a single experience is, however, but a symbol and witness of the larger movement of human conduct whose record makes the history of ethics. What the individual illustrates in the course of his own moral growth, history reports as the evolution of morality, and to observe and distinguish the motives which have been traced as the roots of goodness is the task of the history of ethics. What, then, has ethics to say of these phases of experience which succeed each other in a single life? It is most interesting to observe that each of these successive steps of moral progress has become accepted in the history of ethics as final and satisfying, as though it were not a step but a landing, where the mind might rest. Ethics, that is to say, as expounded by successive masters, reproduces in the form of doctrine what personal experience exhibits as phases of life; and the history of ethics is essentially the story of these successive attempts to give to each mode of conduct the stability of a philosophical creed. The self-assertion of the child, the adjustment of the youth, and the self-discovery of the mature mind,—these, which taken together make a moral autobiography, reappear in the history of ethics under the titles of Egoism,

Prudentialism, and Idealism, and these three schools of opinion represent in the main the theories of conduct which philosophy has described.

"What is my duty?" one asks, as he finds himself set in the world of other people; and the first answer he receives from the history of ethics is that of Egoism. "You have no duty. Assert yourself. Seek your own pleasure. Satisfy your own desire. All else is illusion, misdirected sentiment, and in the end social degeneration." The classical exposition of philosophical Egoism has for many generations been provided by the teaching of Hobbes. "Of the voluntary acts of every man the object is some *good to himself.*"[1] "When a man *deliberates* whether he shall do a thing or not do it, . . . he does nothing else but consider whether it be better for himself to do it or not to do it."[2] "Whatsoever is the object of any man's appetite or desire; that is it which he for his part calleth *good:* and the object of his hate, and aversion, *evil.*"[3] Here is a simple law of conduct, — the frank assertion of self-interest and the outright denial of social obligation. Virtues which are apparently generous or self-forgetting are but disguises of self-consideration. Reverence, teaches Hobbes, is "the conception we have concerning another, that he hath the *power* to do unto us both

---

[1] "Leviathan," Part I, Ch. XIV, "English Works of Thomas Hobbes," ed. Molesworth, 1839, III, p. 120.

[2] "On Liberty and Necessity," "Works," IV, p. 273.

[3] "Leviathan," Part I, Ch. VI, "Works," III, p. 41.

good and *hurt*, but *not* the *will* to do us hurt."[1] Pity is "*imagination* or *fiction* of *future* calamity to *ourselves*, proceeding from the sense of *another* man's calamity."[2] "*Sudden glory*, is the passion which maketh those *grimaces* called LAUGHTER; and is caused either by some sudden act of their own, that pleaseth them; or by the apprehension of some deformed thing in another, by comparison whereof they suddenly applaud themselves."[3] Even "*goodwill*" or "*charity* sometimes called love," is the disguise of a man's consciousness of his own power. "There can be no greater argument to a man, of his own power, than to find himself able not only to accomplish his own desires, but also to *assist* other men in theirs: and this is that conception wherein consisteth charity."[4] Thus the very sentiments, which appear to be indisputable evidences of altruism, are, in fact, evidences of the strategy of selfishness; and the service of others becomes, as has been said of gratitude, "a sense of favors to come."

To the egoism of Hobbes has now succeeded the more modern and virile teaching of Nietzsche, with its persuasive appeal to natural law and to force of will. What Hobbes offers as a refuge of weakness, Nietzsche commends as a mark of strength. Hobbes reverts to an absolute monarchy; Nietzsche proclaims an absolute anarchy.

---

[1] "Human Nature," Ch. VIII, § 7, "Works," IV, p. 40.
[2] "Human Nature," Ch. IX, § 10, "Works," IV, p. 44.
[3] "Leviathan," Part I, Ch. VI, "Works," III, p. 46.
[4] "Human Nature," Ch. IX, § 17, "Works," IV, p. 49.

Where Hobbes would confirm and reënforce morality, Nietzsche would trample on morality and advance beyond good and evil. Yet the law of conduct is in both cases that of an unqualified Egoism. Morality, teaches Nietzsche, "finds its power in a certain art of enchantment on which it relies. . . . It is able to paralyze, or even to win, — often with a single glance, — the critical will; it may even at times convince the will against itself. Ever since men have preached and argued on earth, morality has been the greatest artist of seduction."[1] One must choose in his conduct whether he is to be among those who rule or among those who obey, with the masters or with the slaves. Healthy nations like the Greek have promoted a Master-morality, weak nations like the Hebrew have taught a Slave-morality; and the most degenerate outcome of this creed was the Christian religion, with its praise of humility, sympathy, and sacrifice. Assert thyself then, teaches Nietzsche, as of the master-class. "Life is *essentially* the appropriation, the injury, the subduing of the alien and weak. It is suppression, compulsion, the enforcing of its own forms. It is assimilation, and at the least and gentlest, exploitation."[2] "A social state regarded as sovereign and universal, not as a weapon in the struggle of

[1] "Werke," 1895, 1te Abt., Bd. IV, s. 5, 'Morgenröthe,' 2te Aufl., Vorw., § 3. Cf. the interesting volume of Mencken, "The Philosophy of Friedrich Nietzsche," 1908.
[2] Op. cit., Bd. VII, s. 238, 'Jenseits von Gut und Böse,' 5te Aufl., § 259.

powers, but as a defence against such struggle, . . . as though each will should regard another as its equal, that is a principle which is *hostile to life itself*."¹ "What is happiness? It is the feeling that power *increases*, — that resistance has been overcome. *Not* contentment, but more power; *not* peace, but war; *not* virtue, but efficiency. . . . The weak and crippled should go to the wall: that is the first principle of *our* philanthropy. And one should help them to go.²

The survival of the fit, in other words, is as inevitable in social life as in physical life. To check the action of this principle by any sacrifice of the strong for the weak is to obstruct social progress. Christianity, having taken the part of the weak against the strong, having subordinated the instincts which tend to preserve life, is — Nietzsche teaches — "the One great curse, the One great inward corruption, the One great instinct of revenge, for which no weapon is venomous, clandestine, subterranean, or *mean* enough; — the One ineradicable blot on human nature."³ "Do I counsel you to love your neighbor? I counsel you, rather, to shun your neighbor and to love those farthest away! Above the love of neighbor stands the love of the distant and the future man."⁴

---

[1] Op. cit., Bd. VII, s. 369, 'Zur Genealogie der Moral,' 4te Aufl., § 11.

[2] Op. cit., Bd. VIII, s. 218, 'Der Antichrist,' 1ste Aufl., § 2.

[3] Op. cit., Bd. VIII, s. 313, 'Der Antichrist,' 1ste Aufl., § 62.

[4] Op. cit., Bd. VI, s. 88, 'Also sprach Zarathustra,' 4te Aufl., 1ster Teil.

This unflinching Egoism, with its anticipation of an aristocracy of efficiency, cannot be lightly dismissed as the reckless extravagance of a diseased brain. It is, in fact, nothing less than a rigorous application to human life of the principle of natural selection. Are we essentially animals, contending in a struggle for existence, from which is to emerge a Master-race, or may it be maintained, as Huxley said, that "Social progress means a checking of the cosmic process at every step, and the substitution for it of another which may be called the ethical process; the end of which is not the survival of those who may happen to be the fittest, in respect of the whole of the conditions which obtain, but of those who are ethically the best"?[1] Is it possible to affirm with Fiske that: "When humanity began to be evolved, an entirely new chapter in the history of the universe was opened. Henceforth the life of the nascent soul came to be first in importance, and the bodily life became subordinated to it;"[1] or may the destiny of the individual be detached from that of other people, and social progress be secured at the loss of social sympathy and service? Can there be a survival of the fit which is not accompanied by a revival of the unfit? Is society, that is to say, a chaos or an organism? Is war or peace the ideal state? Are we devourers one of another, or are we members one of another? The philosophy of Nietzsche,

---

[1] "Evolution and Ethics," 1905, p. 31.
[2] "Destiny of Man," 1884, p. 30.

even more than that of Hobbes, is attractive by reason of its simplicity; but life is not so simple as it may seem. The determined effort to be a master in a world of slaves may have as disastrous an issue as the pathetic life of Nietzsche himself. The cynical conversion of the generous virtues into disguises of self-interest in the teaching of Hobbes may blight the very happiness which was the supreme aim. Egoists, it has been lately said, are guilty of a kind of "stupid provinciality." They are like "those closet-philosophers whom Locke describes. 'The truth is, they canton out to themselves a little Goshen in the intellectual world, where light shines and as they conclude, day blesses them; but the rest of that vast expansum they give up to night and darkness, and so avoid coming near it.'"[1]

Thus the paradox of morality becomes restated in its negative form. "If there is one thing more certain than another, it is that to do an action because of the pleasure it brings, is precisely the way to lose the pleasure. Pleasure . . . is exactly that which we must not aim at, if we desire to secure it."[2] The more resolutely, in other words, the egoist sets his face to his predetermined end, the more likely he is to find no pleasure there. Many a man has abandoned the beaten path across the plains of life because he saw in the distance some beckoning happiness, and has found himself pursuing a

[1] Perry, "The Moral Economy," 1909, p. 62.
[2] Courtney, "Constructive Ethics," 1886, p. 89.

vanishing mirage. He has missed not only his end, but his way, and finds himself at last adrift in a trackless world.

Yet even these considerations should not disguise the positive significance of the philosophy of Egoism. Self-interest, even though it lead, when logically pursued, to social anarchy, has its part to play in the creation of morality. The first step in the growth of character is the securing of stability and worth for the single life. To lose oneself one must first possess oneself. To abnegate self is to cut off the root of conduct. The furious protest of Nietzsche against asceticism, and the contempt of Hobbes for self-forgetfulness, have at least this justification. Absolute altruism is moral suicide. Self-interest is not to be abolished but to be educated, just as the baby's outreaching for the world is not to be repressed but to be trained. Indeed, the individual himself, in his moral growth as in his physical growth, discovers new self-interests as life proceeds. The self in which he is interested is not a fixed fact, but a moving process. Within the single self there are several selves, — "a natural Me," as Professor James has said, "a social Me, and a spiritual Me," — and the question of a rational egoism is: Which self am I? Is it the self which I may outgrow, or is it the self which I may attain? To free the higher self from the domination of the lower self; to

"Move upward, working out the beast,
And let the ape and tiger die;" —

this process may itself leave one within the limits of a philosophy of Egoism, but it is none the less the essential starting-point on the way to moral maturity.

When one passes from the ethics of Egoism to the ethics of Prudentialism, he enters a region in which ordinary conduct finds itself more at home. To conclude with Hobbes that all virtues are but disguised forms of selfishness; to believe with Nietzsche that "One must learn to love himself . . . with a wholesome and healthy love, so that one is sufficient to himself, and does not run about in ways which are described as love of one's neighbor,"[1] — all this may seem the mere inebriety of philosophy; but the balancing of expediency and the measuring of utility may well appear the marks of sobriety and worldly wisdom. The inquirer for a law of conduct turns, therefore, with a more reasonable hope to the prudentialist with his question: "What is my duty?" and the philosopher of Prudentialism, surveying a world where pleasure must be sought and pain avoided, yet where each increase of pleasure may involve to others corresponding pain, replies, "You must calculate your duty. Secure that pleasure which gives least pain to others; banish that pain which does not serve the larger pleasure." "Weigh pains, weigh pleasures," said Bentham, "and as the balance stands, will stand the question of right and wrong."

[1] Op. cit., Bd. VI, s. 282, 'Also sprach Zarathustra,' 3ter Teil, § 2.

"Vice may be defined to be a miscalculation of chances: a mistake in estimating the value of pleasures and pains. It is false moral arithmetic."[1] Mill has thus summarized this view: "Bentham's idea of the world is that of a collection of persons pursuing each his separate interest or pleasure, and the prevention of whom from jostling one another more than is unavoidable, may be attempted by hopes and fears derived from three sources, — the law, religion, and public opinion."[2] Thus the individual, while no longer proposing for himself the hopeless venture of an isolated happiness, still finds in the social order a risk to that happiness. Over against his own aim stands the not less justifiable happiness of others, and between the two a balance of expediency must be struck. The person and the social good sit, as it were, on opposite ends of a tilt. If one end goes down, the other goes up; and the problem of morality is to keep the balance true.

Spencer has reduced this problem of the social equilibrium to a mathematical formula. Conduct, he says, is primarily directed to the maintenance or prolongation of life. The primary instinct is the instinct to live; the first test of conduct is its contribution to life. "Along with this greater elaboration of life produced by the pursuit of more numerous ends, there goes that increased duration of life which constitutes the supreme

---

[1] "Deontology," 1834, I, pp. 131, 137.
[2] "Dissertations and Discussions," 1859, I, p. 362.

end."[1] What pleasure is to the egoist, life is to the evolutionist. The formula for conduct is thus originally simple. That which prolongs life is good. The reward of duty-doing is the promise of the Psalmist: "With long life will I satisfy him."[2] The test of wisdom is that which the Book of Proverbs offers: "Length of days is in her right hand."[3]

This rule of conduct, however, as Spencer immediately points out, is soon found to be insufficient. Though one may prize length of days, he prizes many other things even more. Life is not to be reckoned as mere duration. Quality counts not less than quantity. Some lives, though short, are full; and some, though long, are empty. "Honorable age is not that which standeth in length of time, nor that is measured by number of years. But wisdom is the gray hair unto men, and an unspotted life is old age."[4] "Better fifty years of Europe than a cycle of Cathay," said Tennyson; better, that is to say, a short life, rich in breadth and depth, than a long life, poor or narrow in experience or interest. Spencer states this modification of his original thesis in his favorite language of biology. "An oyster," he says, "may live longer than a cuttle-fish . . . but the sum of vital activities is far less in the oyster than in the cuttle-fish." Thus the original law of conduct needs amplification. To duration

---

[1] "Data of Ethics," 1879, Ch. II: "The Evolution of Conduct," p. 14.   [2] Ps. xci. 16.   [3] Prov. iii. 16.   [4] Wisdom iv. 8, 9.

of life must be added the further element of complexity. The moral formula must include not only length of conduct but breadth. "Estimating life," Spencer therefore concludes, "by multiplying its length into its breadth, we must see that the augmentation of it which accompanies evolution of conduct, results from increase of both factors." Moral arithmetic, in other words, is applied to obtain the maximum of duration consistent with the maximum of quality and depth. Fulness of life is the product of length of days by breadth of experience. The good life is the result of a prudent computation. It refuses the career of an oyster, though it promise length of days; it accepts the vicissitudes which await the cuttle-fish, for the sake of the "vital activities" which are to be enjoyed.

Here is a principle of conduct much more likely than a philosophy of Egoism to commend itself to the normal mind. It at least recognizes the conditions under which the moral problem must be solved. It attempts no isolation of personal happiness from the world of common good, no moral anarchism, or, as Nietzsche called his creed, "immoralism." Round the person is seen the world of other persons, hostile and restrictive indeed, yet compelling consideration. Ethics has become a social science. The question of duty is a social question. A great step has been taken in the evolution of morality when the simple formula of self-interest is thus enriched and complicated by the recognition of social relations and demands.

Prudentialism has also the further merit of representing the ordinary motives of average life, so that its teachings have in them an appearance of sanity, sagacity, and worldly wisdom. It does not ask too much of human nature; it accepts the friction of the world as inevitable and makes itself as comfortable as circumstances permit. Its way is along the level high-road where a great part of the conduct of the world goes about its affairs. Few persons are consistently and irretrievably egoists, but most persons are habitually prudentialists. They compute the consequences of conduct to themselves and to others and establish an equilibrium between obligation and rights. They have outgrown the babyhood of ethics and have realized the social environment of morality. Their moral problem is not approached as if in a vacuum, but as a form of adjustment to the pressure of an inevitable world. Prudentialism is thus a practicable faith, on the level of worldly expediency.

When, however, one is called — as every life is some day called — to go up from this level of a well-considered prudence to the higher region of moral decisions, where the supreme issues of life are to be met, what becomes of the sagacious guidance of this prudentialist creed? It fails one just when it is most needed. It is at home along the high-road, but it does not know the path to the hills. It has no language to interpret conduct precisely when conduct most needs interpretation.

It comes to a point where, instead of quality in life supplementing its quantity, quality has supplanted quantity. The heroism of the instant demands the sacrifice of the future; the call of duty silences the computation of expediency; and at this point prudentialism halts, as at the brink of unexplored adventures and risks. The two factors of Spencer's formula are seen to be incommensurate. When these higher tests of character are reached, no conceivable prolongation of life can atone for lack of quality. Indeed, the longer one may live, the more intolerable life may be, if it be haunted by the recollection of a moral opportunity unused, or a moral crisis shunned. At such times, when the great temptation is to be met, or the noble deed to be done, — at the times, in other words, when morality reaches its most unequivocal expression, — the prudential standard breaks under the strain precisely when conduct most needs support. The choice between life in terms of length and life in terms of breadth is seen to be nothing else than a choice between a moral surrender and a moral victory.

No sooner does one scrutinize any case of moral heroism than he observes this breakdown of prudentialism. At the entrance to the playground of Harvard University, for example, stands a monument, commemorating three young men who died for their country, and in whose name the spot is known as the "Soldiers Field." On the shaft of this monument, inscribed for successive genera-

tions of American youths to read, are these lines
of Emerson : —

> "Though love repine and reason chafe,
> I heard a voice without reply,
> 'Tis man's perdition to be safe
> If for the truth he ought to die."

Noble though these verses may be as poetry, do they,
the inquirer into ethics asks, give judicious counsel
to young men? Is it a sane rule of life which pre-
scribes so rash a sacrifice? To the prudential
moralist the words may well seem little less than
madness. What is this voice without reply which
rebukes the computation of expediency? How
can it be perdition to be safe if length of life be
the original end of conduct? If those young men
of the Civil War had restrained themselves from
such exaggerated sentimentalism, they might have
been alive to-day. Emerson's lines may be better
poetry than Goldsmith's, but was not Goldsmith
more sagacious when he wrote : —

> "For he who fights and runs away,
> May live to fight another day;
> But he who is in battle slain
> Can never rise and fight again."

It is the same paradox of conduct which perplexed
Dante as he journeyed through Purgatory,

> "How can it be that boon distributed
> The more possessors can more wealthy make
> Therein, than if by few it be possessed?"

and the answer of the paradox is that of Virgil,

> "For these, as much the more as one says *Our*,
> So much the more of good each one possesseth,
> And the more people thitherward aspire.
> More are there to love well, and more they love them,
> And, as a mirror, one reflects the other."[1]

The history of conduct abounds in illustrations of this defiance of prudentialism. The Roman general Regulus, to cite a classical case, is made prisoner at Carthage, and released on parole to sue for peace. He returns to Rome, and instead of advising peace, urges a renewal of war. Keeping his parole, however, he surrenders himself to the enemy whose hope he has defeated, and is put to death at Carthage by torture. How shall this conduct of Regulus be estimated? Is it a case of moral heroism worthy of the world's permanent admiration, or is it, on the other hand, to be condemned as Quixotic and extravagant? The same question is raised by many a modern instance, where conduct, instead of "weighing pain" and "weighing pleasure," hears "a voice without reply." All sorts and conditions of men obey this imperative command, the simple not less than the wise, the young quite as unhesitatingly as the old, as though the impulse of obedience came from a deeper source than either education or experience could disclose. The steamship *Cymric*, to cite a case from contemporary life, is on its way to

---

[1] "Purgatory," XV, tr. Longfellow.

Boston, and meets a burning vessel. The sea runs so high that rescue seems impracticable, but the captain reluctantly permits a volunteer crew to launch a boat, and in three journeys, back and forth across a mile of foam, the shipwrecked crew at last is saved. A year later the boatswain, who chose the boat's crew and pulled its stroke oar, is modestly telling his story, and as though it were a self-evident part of his experience, says, " The hardest work of all was to wait until we had leave to go." What has the ethics of prudentialism to say of words like these? They must seem the record of an excited moment, when rational prudence was forgotten in the madness of adventure. To what reasonable man could it be a hard duty to wait at a vessel's rail instead of plunging into a boiling sea?

The force of the new motive becomes even more impressive when the voice without reply is heard, not in any dramatic or conspicuous call, but in the simple course of one's daily duty. In the *London Spectator*, for example, there appeared some years ago the following paragraph: " The medical world has reason to be proud of one of its members who died this week, as the consequence of a really heroic act performed in the course of his professional duty. Dr. Samuel Rabbeth, a young man of only twenty-seven years, senior residential medical officer of the Royal Free Hospital, Gray's Inn Road, found, on Friday fortnight, that a child of four years of age, on whom tracheotomy had been performed to relieve the breathing, must die of diphtheria unless the suffocating membrane was sucked away through a tube; and he risked and lost his life through diphtheria in the attempt to save the child's, which he did not succeed in saving at all. The risk was not one which professional etiquette in any way required him to run, but he ran it in the enthusiasm of his love for service, and he ought to be remembered as one of the noblest martyrs of duty." This comment of the editor was followed the next week by these verses: —

> "It was an offering rare that thou didst yield
> To this poor world and Him who died for thee.
> Few nobler deeds of service have been wrought
> Since the great sacrifice upon the tree.
>
>   *   *   *   *   *   *
>
> "No cry of battle, rousing thy young blood,
> Urged thee to valorous deeds, and hope of fame;
> Lowly to abjectness, thy loving task,
> Humble thy path, unknown till now thy name.
>
>   *   *   *   *   *   *
>
> "Had the child lived, for whom thy life was spent,
> We think we had not grudged the bitter cost.
> But both have died; and some will say, in vain
> Thy calm, heroic spirit has been lost.
>
>   *   *   *   *   *   *
>   .   .   .   .   .   .
>
> "And yet, perchance, beyond the veil of sense,
> At our poor folly, angels may have smiled,
> Seeing a young man enter perfect life,
> And in his arms, a little living child."

Though one can hardly read without a thrill of pride of this act of heroism, can it be, after all, rationally justified? Calmly considered, was it an act on which the angels should smile? Should it not rather be regarded with a smile of pity or scorn? What right had such a youth to risk his life where professional etiquette had not required it? Ought he to be regarded as a martyr of duty, or should he be regarded as a foolhardy enthusiast? What is it which prompts such acts — and similar acts occur every day in the ordinary practice of medicine, and in a thousand exigencies of modern life — and makes them defensible, not to say praiseworthy and noble? One sets these types of conduct before the philosophy of Egoism, and the egoist simply retreats from them as inexplicable or insane. Self-interest may carry one a long way toward self-display or self-respect, but self-interest cannot lurk beneath acts which have neither notoriety nor reward. The desire to shine, the hope of glory, the lust of victory, may sustain a soldier in a dangerous charge, but they can play no part in the equally dangerous and wholly undramatic heroism of the physician bending over his task. This was the kind of conduct against which Nietzsche fairly shrieked his scorn. "Sympathy," he said, "opposes, in the main, the law of development which is the law of *Selection*. It preserves what is ripe for destruction, it operates to defend the disinherited and condemned among men. . . . This disheartening and contagious instinct . . . is

... a chief instrument in the advance of *decadence*."[1] In a characteristic passage the same apostle of "immoralism" maintains that the preaching of such sympathy by Jesus of Nazareth was one evidence of his immaturity and youth. "He died too soon. If he had lived to my age [Nietzsche was then 38], he would have renounced his teaching."[2]

Again, one sets these acts of heroism before the philosophy of Prudentialism, and a still more instructive inconsistency appears. For even though such conduct may be approved by Prudentialism, it must be regarded as lying quite beyond the proper sphere of obligation. Morality is to be discovered by computation, but the very essence of these acts is in their uncalculating and spontaneous character. To compute the chances is to let the chance go by. The soldier in the battle, the locomotive-engineer suddenly confronted by the burning bridge, the sailor sighting the wreck, the doctor at the crisis of his case, cannot stop to weigh pleasure and to weigh pain. The habitual discipline of their callings has developed in them an instinct of loyalty. They hear a voice without reply. They are led by a categorical command, which steadies their wills and to disobey which is moral recreancy.

What is this new principle of conduct, permitting acts which under other rules of life may seem folly or madness, and surrounding one with a new hori-

[1] Op. cit., Bd. VIII, s. 222, 223, 'Der Antichrist,' 1te Aufl., § 7.
[2] Op. cit., Bd. VI, s. 107, 'Also sprach Zarathustra,' 1ster Teil.

zon of obligation, as though he had ascended to a height where a new flora grew, and a fresher air were breathed? This is that summit of philosophy where one falls in with the teachings of ethical idealism. As one recalls these acts of moral heroism, they are seen to occur through loyalty to an ideal,—the ideal of one's duty, or one's vocation, or one's country, or one's God. The ideal which is so commanding presents itself, not as an attainment or achievement, but rather as an unattained or unrealized perfection. The flag of one's country, for example, is not the symbol of one's real country, with its follies and sins, its politics and trade, but the symbol of one's ideal country, the nation which is as yet nothing but a hope; yet in the presence of this symbol of an ideal, this witness of a dream, many a man has found it perdition to be safe, and a joy to die. The Kingdom of God for which Christians pray is not a perfect world which actually exists, or is even likely to exist; yet the Christian Church survives by faith in that ideal, and is nurtured by that prayer. It is the same with each humble act of moral heroism. Regulus is loyal to his ideal of patriotism; the *Cymric's* boatswain to his ideal of service; the young English doctor to the ideal of his profession. Moral philosophy must either retreat from its own problem precisely when this problem becomes most clarified and supreme, or must take account of conduct as it mounts to these heights of character and looks out over a new world.

And here the student of ethics finds himself touching that golden thread which runs through the whole history of philosophy, and unites many masters in the faith of ethical idealism. Whether it be Plato, counselling that: "The movement of the soul be turned from the world of becoming into that of being . . . and of the highest and best of being, or in other words, of the good"[1]; or Paul's confession: "I was not disobedient unto the heavenly vision"[2]; or the Imperative of Kant: "Act on that maxim only which thou canst at the same time will to become a universal law"[3]; or Green's statement of the end of conduct, as "desired, because conceived as absolutely desirable"[4]; — in all these teachings the command of duty is accepted, not as provisional, but as absolute, "a voice without reply." "Man has definite capabilities, the realization of which . . . form his True Good. They are not realized, however, in any life. . . . Yet goodness is proportionate to the habitual responsiveness to the idea of there being such a True Good."[5] The Moral Ideal, that is to say, though itself unrealized, opens the path to reality; and though itself visionary, rescues from illusion. The prudential theory of morals induced Spencer to conclude that the sense of obligation

---

[1] "Republic," VII, 518; tr. Jowett, III, 218.

[2] Acts xxvi, 19.

[3] "Grundlegung z. Metaphysik d. Sitten," Werke, ed. 1903, IV, 421.

[4] "Prolegomena of Ethics," 1883, p. 203.

[5] Green, op. cit., pp. 189, 190.

was a survival which would disappear as life became more adjusted to its environing world. "The sense of duty," he says, "is transitory, and will diminish as fast as moralization increases. . . . With complete adaptation to the social state, that element in the moral consciousness which is expressed by the word 'obligation' will disappear."[1] The ethical idealist reaches precisely the opposite conclusion. To him the sense of obligation, instead of being a survival, is a prophecy. Instead of diminishing with moral development, it becomes more imperative. The idealist, instead of floundering in the slippery places of self-interest, or trudging along the flat country of calculated pleasure, climbs to the heights of moral decision, and finds his path already explored by the most trustworthy guides. His way leads, not to illusion and obscurity, but to insight and reality. Human nature welcomes this ascent. "Man is an ideal-forming animal."[2] "Ethics leads back to the essential nature of man and that in its turn leads to the absolute principle of things."[3]

Here, then, is an answer to the problem of conduct which the student of the Social Question must approach with peculiar interest and hope. It reproduces, in the language of philosophy, the same story of the moral process, which has already been told in the language of personal growth. What a moral biography reports as happening at

[1] "Data of Ethics," 1879, p. 127.
[2] Grote, "A Treatise on the Moral Ideals," 1876, p. 392.
[3] Courtney, "Constructive Ethics," 1886, p. 12.

maturity, now presents itself as the maturity of ethics. The same moral paradox, the same self-discovery through loyalty and self-realization in self-surrender, which marks the ripening of individual experience, marks the ethical creed of idealism. The same appearance of exaggeration and vagueness, which delayed the moral maturity of the single life, still repels the egoist and the prudentialist. The same fluid conception of morality reappears. It is not a choice between fixed alternatives, but a growth, like that from childhood to manhood, where each phase of experience has its justification and makes its contribution, but where the meaning of the process is disguised until its end is reached. The stream of conduct has many windings and eddies as it follows the channels of self-interest or expediency, but its natural movement sweeps it toward idealism as a river broadens to the sea.

A justification of ethical idealism seems likely, therefore, to be at the same time an interpretation of the Social Question. For here, also, the dominant motives of humanity, pity, sympathy, and hope are not easily justified by the creeds of Egoism or Prudentialism. Here, also, self-interest and expediency obstruct and delay the better social order; and here, also, the idealist sees his vision and dreams his dream. If, therefore, the Social Question is an ethical question, it may also be true that its progress is to be a further reproduction of the same moral process which has been traced, first in the experiences of the individual, and then in the history of the race, and which fulfils itself in moral idealism. Such a conclusion would seem to put a key of the Social Question into one's hands. This vast and complex social movement which agitates the mind of the present age, would be, from this point of view, approached as a case of ethics written upon the page of contemporary life. Each social problem, — the family, the industrial order, and the State, — would repeat the story of the moral process, and report once more the same struggle of moral types, and the gradual emergence, through self-interest and expediency, of a practical and constructive faith in ethical idealism.

V

ETHICAL IDEALISM AND THE SOCIAL QUESTION

THE first difficulty met by the student of ethical idealism is created by its appearance of remoteness and intangibility. Egoism, however limited its vision, has, as it were, its feet on the ground, and runs no risk of missing its way. Human beings are, after all, animals, with brutal instincts and greedy ambitions, and to recognize without flinching the merciless struggle for mastery seems at least a virile, candid, and unashamed attitude of mind. Prudentialism also, however commercial its aim, has at least an appearance of sagacity and practicability, as though adapted to a world of shrewd business dealings, where the ethics of trade make the best rule of life. Idealism, on the other hand, may easily appear to view life, as it were, from a distance, where cold facts are softened and gross motives veiled. Choice spirits, like Plato and Kant, may thus survey the world from the calm heights of philosophy; but plain people, it may seem, must live among the scrambling and competing multitude, whose ruling motives Hobbes and Nietzsche, Bentham and Spencer, have more accurately described. Yet, curiously enough, it is precisely this remoteness and inaccessibility which, throughout the whole history of human thought, have given to idealism its commanding solicitation. It is like a mountain which invites exploration, but remains unconquered. Though its peak be inaccessible, it provokes the desire to climb; and as one mounts, though he may never reach the summit, he has the world at his feet. What seemed a tangle of meaninglessness when seen from below, gets perspective when seen from above. The flat and prosaic fall into their places in the broader view. Not illusion, but horizon, is the reward of the idealist. Not until one discovers in his experience this intermingling of prophecy and fact, of vision and task, of the call to the ideal and fidelity to the real, has the meaning of life become plain, or the way of life straight.

To overcome, then, this primary difficulty of idealism one has but to recognize that the same experience of a beckoning reality and an expanding horizon is repeated at many points. The moral process is not exceptional or unique. Wherever the ascent of life is made, whether toward Truth, or Beauty, or Goodness, the same succession of steps is taken, and the same elusiveness and inaccessibility are disclosed. Science, art, and morals are alike in this, that each is solicited by an unscaled height. Absolute Truth, perfected Beauty, unmixed Goodness, — all these alike are not attainments, but ideals. Whether it be the intellect, or the imagination, or the will, which is summoned to its best, the call to the heights is the call of the Ideal.

Such, for instance, is the history of the mind on its way to Truth, — the story of the evolution of the scholar. One may not, at first, recognize this appeal of the ideal. Instead of lifting his eyes to the hills, he fixes them on the ground and walks along the level of an intellectual Egoism or an intellectual Prudentialism. Truth is estimated for its contribution to self-interest; Truth is balanced against the other desires of life. A trader may value Truth for what it will buy; a schoolboy may resist the attack of Truth in an attitude of self-defence. "What is the teacher talking about?" asks one boy of another; and his playmate answers: "I have not the least idea; I just let him teach." Finally, from these experiences of self-interest and self-adjustment there emerges a new habit of mind. It is the mind of the scholar. And what is a scholar? It is he to whom truth is neither a tool to use, nor a task to meet, but an ideal to obey. It is not the truth which he has attained which persuades the scholar's mind; it is the truth which he has not attained. He gives himself to truths, because of his faith in Truth. The truths he studies are many; the Truth he seeks is one. Truths shut him in, but the Truth liberates him, so that he becomes a liberally educated man. The Truth, in the great words of the fourth Gospel, makes him free. Thus the scholar is an idealist.

He is, as Fichte said, a priest of Truth; he ministers before the Truth as before an altar. There are many truths which a schoolboy knows better than a scholar, but the scholar is distinguished from the schoolboy by his attitude toward truth. The Truth to him is an ideal. He dedicates himself to a segment of truth because of his faith in the circle of Truth. If he knew the whole truth, it would be a consistent whole; and each fragment of the truth is precious because it has its part in the organism of reality.

Here is the justification of those laws of reasoning which we call logic. Logic is an evidence of this faith that truth is consistent and whole. Logical error means, not that the statement is absurd, but that it does not fit in with other statements to make a consistent unity. I may maintain, for example, that two and two make five, if I do not attach this proposition to other aspects of truth. The error arises when one such statement is set with others in a logical world. Its association with the whole of truth convicts it of falsity. The scholar's ideal of the unity of Truth becomes his test of each fragment of truth. As he ascends the heights of the Ideal, the real falls into place before his eyes.

The same story may be told, again, in terms of the imagination, and the evolution of the artist traced along the same road with the evolution of the scholar. What are the possible relations of the mind toward beauty? This end, also, may first be approached in terms of self-interest. Beauty may be a source of profit, or an object of trade. The organ-grinder manufactures music for the sake of pennies. His business is with art, but he is a mechanic, not an artist. The palette-grinder uses the colors with which the artist paints, but the palette-grinder is not the artist; and we are amused when he says of his coöperative labors: "He and I painted that picture; I mixed the colors and he laid them on." The organist and the organ-blower combine to play the anthem, but we are again amused when the organ-blower wipes his brow and says: "Did we not play that well!" Or, once more, the mind turned toward the Beautiful may approach it in the attitude of the Prudentialist. Beauty is recognized but is not appropriated. The weary tourist in the picture-gallery may hold himself on the defensive against the attack of art. He will see as much as his fatigue can endure, and as little as his self-respect will permit. He estimates art, not by its appeal to his imagination, but by the judgments of his guide-book; like a tired woman at the St. Louis Fair, who had just vitality enough to read her well-thumbed catalogue and announce that the picture before her was owned by Corot and was painted by George Gould. Finally, through this process of æsthetic education there emerges a new creation. It is the mind of the artist. And what is the artist? The artist is an idealist. He lives in the presence and under the perpetual persuasion of an unrealized, yet imperative Beauty. What he creates is but the symbol of his ideal; yet it is his ideal which makes him able to create. The light of the ideal shines upon his material and makes it beautiful. As Lowell said of the musician: "He builds a bridge from dreamland to his lay." The problem of art is thus the suggestion of the ideal by the description of the real. Millet sees two peasants in a ploughed field saying their prayers, and paints them in their uncouth and rugged simplicity; but the homely scene becomes a parable of life because it is touched with the ideal of a human and patient faith. Raphael sees an Italian woman coming down a narrow lane with a baby in her arms, and paints her as she comes; but he sets round this human figure a cloud of angels, and the peasant is transfigured into the Virgin bearing the Holy Child from heaven to earth; and the beholder sits reverently in the little room in Dresden before the ideal of religious art.

Precisely analogous with these experiences in the evolution of the scholar and the artist is the emergence of idealism in the evolution of the Duty-doer. Here, also, one may defy the world of other people, or may adjust himself to that world; and there are many incidents of conduct which easily fall under either rule. Through these conventional rules of conduct, however, there breaks at times the vision of the ideal, and as the scholar responds to the ideal of Truth, and the artist to the ideal of Beauty, so the Duty-doer is called by his ideal to the doing of his best. Indeed, the moral ideal is not only analogous with the intellectual and æsthetic ideals, but is an essential element in both. The scholar is not secure from his own intellectual risks until his scholarship is fortified by his ethical idealism. The unmoralized scholar, the self-seeking or prudential scholar, may easily miss the finer qualities of the truth itself. There are moral conditions of scholarly achievement. Intellectual acuteness is not a sufficient substitute for intellectual morality. A scholar must be not only creative, but sincere. The pure in heart, it is written, shall see God. Their undefiled character gives them not only a finer morality, but a finer insight. Their eyes are clear because their hearts are clean. If Kepler could say that an undevout astronomer was mad, with much more justice it may be said that an unclean man of science is blind. The scientific spirit, indeed, generates, through its own demands, this ethical sensitiveness. "There is a morality," Tyndall said, "brought to bear upon such matters which, in point of severity, is probably without a parallel in any other domain of intellectual action. The desire for anything but the truth must be absolutely annihilated; and to attain perfect accuracy no labour must be shirked, no difficulty ignored."[1]

The same correlation holds between the moral ideal and the æsthetic ideal. Art for art's sake, it has been urged, is a sufficient creed for the artist. The beautiful however naked, the fair however foul, is an adequate theme for literature

[1] "Sound," 1st ed., 1873, p. 26.

or art. To deny this "immoralism" of the modern realist is not to insist that art should be always preaching or literature always lecturing. Life is a sufficient problem without problem-plays, and beauty needs no accessories to point out its lesson. Art makes its appeal not to action, but to appreciation.[1] Yet, these very qualities of art have their moral conditions. Veracity, insight, nobility, spirituality, are all parts of the beauty to which the nature of man responds. Art for art's sake, the sensual without the spiritual, the flesh without the soul, has been, in many periods of history, not the sign of æsthetic promise, but the mark of a decadent art. Art in the Golden Age of Greece was the handmaid of Greek religion and the instrument of Greek idealism; and when art became detached from the ideals of Truth and Goodness, the decline of Greek art began. "Let our artists," said Plato, "rather be those who are gifted to discern the true nature of beauty and grace; then will our youth dwell in a land of health, amid fair sights and sounds; and beauty, the effluence of fair works, will meet the sense like a breeze, and insensibly draw the soul even in childhood into harmony with the beauty of reason."[2] The Moral Ideal, that is to say, is not merely coördinate with the ideals which create

---

[1] See the admirable chapter in Perry, op. cit., on "The Moral Criticism of Fine Art."

[2] "The Dialogues of Plato," tr. Jowett, 1871, "Republic," III, 401.

science and art, but it participates in their creative work and affirms the unity of the life of the spirit. "Duty," in Emerson's perfect aphorism, "is one thing with science, with beauty, and with joy."

Such are the analogies of the spiritual life which confirm the faith of the idealist. A large part of human experience is unquestionably preoccupied with the things which one has, and this possession of the real is often a repression of the ideal. The motives which give beauty and strength to character proceed, on the contrary, not so much from the things one has, as from the things which one has not; from what an English philosopher has called "*Egence*,"[1] or the consciousness of an unrealized desire. These higher compulsions do not push from below, but draw from above. They confirm the teaching of Jesus: "No man cometh unto me, except the Father draw him." They are the evidence, not of things which are seen, but of things which are not seen. "Human life and conduct," Jowett said at the close of his Introduction to the "Republic,"[2] "are affected by ideals in the same way that they are affected by the example of eminent men. Neither the one nor the other is immediately applicable in practice, but there is a virtue flowing from them which tends to raise individuals above the common routine of society and

---

[1] Grote, op. cit., p. 30: "Egence, and difference of egence, are the great facts of the universe."
[2] Amer. ed., 1885, p. 162.

trade." Idealism, in short, though hidden from large areas of experience, as a mountain is hidden by lower and nearer hills, discloses its height and challenges the climber as he ascends. Successive peaks appear, receding but persuading, unseen by the dwellers in the valleys, but beckoning to those who dare to climb.

These large and abstract considerations of the nature of Goodness may appear to have slight connection with the pressing and concrete problems which create the Social Question. What, one may ask, has the modern problem of the family, or poor-relief, or industrial adjustment, or political reform, to do with these high doctrines of Plato or Kant, or with these spiritual affinities of Truth, Beauty, and Goodness? Have we not risen in these ethical discussions far above the prosaic facts of social life, as a mountain-climber leaves below him the noises of a busy town? When, however, one reconsiders the nature of the Social Question and recalls its poignant note of moral passion and need, it becomes evident that nothing less than the entire story of ethics can cover the entire movement of social change. The Social Question is not a fragment of modern morality, but the summary of it; not an eddy in the stream of modern goodness, but the main current in which that goodness flows. It is not, therefore, until the good life is followed all the way from its source to its end that the ultimate direction of the Social Question is revealed. It is not until the path of ethics is climbed to its summit that the world below is seen with perspective and precision. The abstractions of ethics lead, not to remoteness and detachment, but to discernment and horizon. The chief source of perplexity in the Social Question is in seeing it from below; the chief source of courage in the Social Question is in seeing it from above. What is it, then, which is thus seen as one looks down upon the Social Question from the heights of ethical idealism? It becomes evident, from this point of view, not only that the Social Question is in its form and language an ethical question, but that, in its path and progress also, it follows the same way which ethics has explored. Each form which the Social Question assumes exhibits the same succession of alternatives, and the same process of enlargement, which the theory of ethics illustrates. Each phase of the Social Question is an attempt to solve the problem of the person within the social order, first in terms of Egoism, then in terms of Prudentialism, and finally in terms of Idealism; and in each case the process is retarded and the movement remains unfulfilled, until ethical idealism expresses itself in social action and the person realizes himself in the common good.

Here is the end toward which the whole course of the present inquiry has led. The various social questions restate in the language of the present age the story of ethics. Through the materialism and commercialism of the time there is slowly emerging a practical faith in moral idealism, and, in so far as this faith is realized in works, the Social Question may be approached with sanity, confidence, and hope. It finds itself concerned, not with a fixed condition permitting an immediate and final remedy, but with a movement, a growth, a way of life. Each increase in social responsibility, each fragment of effective social service contributes to this social idealism; and to trace this process, and weigh and estimate its various steps, to recognize and promote this emergence of idealism, is the approach of philosophy to the problems of modern life. The theory of ethics, in other words, puts into one's hand a master-key, which not only unlocks the main gate of the Social Question, but admits one to the meaning of its separate parts; and as the ethical idealist fits his key into these successive doors, they open easily from room to room.

One approaches, for example, the most immediate and fundamental of social problems, — the institution of the family. It is the vestibule of the social order, the unit of civilization, the original group into which, by the very circumstances of human birth and infancy, each individual is introduced. In one aspect this social institution may be regarded as an instrument for the satisfaction of self-interest, and in another aspect it is an arrangement of mutual convenience and advantage. Egoism, both of the flesh and of the spirit, has created many a family; Prudentialism has made of the family what is known to the law as a contract, "between the two parties concerned," with all the temporariness and reservations of any business contract. The history of the family confirms at many points both these views of its origin and intention. Polygamy identifies the family with the egoism of the male; polyandry establishes a unity in terms of the female. The evolution of the family is a curious record of this struggle of types, in which every possible relation between man and woman has been historically tried and sifted out, so that the fittest might survive. The family still remains in many minds a piece of property or form of trade, whose ethics must be those of personal gain or of the balance of pleasures; and it is precisely because the ethics of the family is so often interpreted under the creeds of Egoism or of Prudentialism that the crisis in the history of domestic life, which now confronts the world, has arrived. Instability in the family is not chiefly, as is often fancied, the result of imperfect legislation or of economic change; it occurs, most of all, through the survival in the family of the rudimentary instincts from which morality sprang—the egoistic instincts of the beast or the baby, the prudential instincts of the trader or the speculator.

And meantime, what is the conception of the family which through the long ages of its evolution has gradually emerged, and which is now the only guarantee of its stability and permanence? It is the conception of this social institution as an expression of Idealism. The family, many people may be almost surprised to learn, is not a device invented to procure either personal happiness or mutual convenience. The family is, on the contrary, the world's first and greatest venture in altruism. Its permanent foundation is nothing less than a self-forgetting love, which gives itself to its partner without computation of gain. The family is in danger when it is created for what one can get out of it; and it is safe only when it is prized for what one can give to it. The family is the chief human instrument for the socializing of the will and the spiritualizing of desire. He who loses his life in the family, alone finds it. Self-surrender to the family is the only path to self-realization within the family.

Nothing is more curious than to observe this idealism as it operates in ordinary and commonplace people when they approach the formation of a family. To the looker-on there may be little that is attractive in either the man or the woman who together form the union. Each of them may have foibles, and neither may have charm. Yet the essence of the union lies in the discovery by each partner of virtues and graces which are perhaps unpossessed, but which are striven for and desired. It is this idealizing of each other which holds them both together for better or worse. Each member of a family must accept his fellow-member not for what he is, but for what he wants to be. To live on the level of actual character is to live in an earthquake-zone of constant agitation and imminent disaster. The ideal of the family is the security of the family. The most important step in the education of the human race is taken, when out of the surviving instincts of animalism and commercialism there emerges, in a man and a woman, this ideal of a humanized love, dedicated to the creation of a family, and finding in that union, not limitation but enlargement, not sacrifice but joy. In a word, the family is a record of ethical idealism written on the pages of human history, and the rupture of the family is a reversion to ethical types from which the evolution of morality has slowly and laboriously emerged.

The same key, which thus opens the door to the meaning of the family, may be applied to each of the larger social groups of which the family is a part. One passes through this vestibule of the social order into the life of the community, or of the industrial world, or of the State, and at each point the story of ethics repeats itself in the language of the modern world. At the very door of this common life, for example, one meets the tragic contrasts of poverty and prosperity, and asks for direction to an effective principle of charity. What is one's duty to the poor? How shall the individual realize himself within the social circle of diverse conditions and pitiful needs? He may try, in the first place, the answer of the egoist. He has no duty to the poor. Social classes owe to each other nothing. Let the weak go to the wall, and let the strong survive. But what is the consequence of this social cynicism? The more one thus retreats from social obligation, the more directly he contributes to social disaster. Heartlessness breeds hopelessness, and hopelessness in its turn begets recklessness and revolution. Egoism is thus not only a retreat from philanthropy, but a defeat of self-interest itself. If the strong would survive in a social world, they must learn to serve. "He that would be greatest among you, let him be your minister."

A second and more defensible attitude toward the problem of poverty is that of the prudentialist. He conforms to the social conditions of personal welfare. He will not pave his path to happiness with the bodies of the fallen. He consents to the taxation and legislation which check disorder and reduce pauperism as menaces to social peace. Here, it must be admitted, is the motive which prompts a large proportion of the operations of charity. It is administered as a protective system, a social police-force, a prevention of contagion, both physical and moral; or, as was said of one ostentatious giver, as a form of fire-insurance taken out against the risks of the next world. Prudentialism, thus applied to the problem of poverty, may carry a community a long way towards scientific relief. It is discovered one day, for instance, that garments sewed in unsanitary tenements are worn by prosperous women in luxurious homes, so that disease reaches its hand across the great city and teaches the solidarity of society in the tragic language of contagion and death. Improved housing, therefore, the cleansing of the slums, the crusade against tuberculosis, the suppression of sweat-shops, the inspection of trade, are all promoted by an enlightened prudence.

Yet, while expediency has its part in directing the operations of charity, it cannot supply the motives which give to charity its continuity and its happiness. Charity, though it may repay the giver in personal security or in peace of mind, is not charity because it pays. It is charity because it expresses that old-fashioned and perennial motive of humanity, which the New Testament calls Love. Charity, in other words, is the attempt to find a place in modern statesmanship, civic administration, trade, and personal life, for the ideals of humanity, fraternity, and social peace. It is one aspect of the emergence of ethical idealism; one utterance of the social conscience of the time. The aims of charity are never completely fulfilled; the hopes which sustain it are never wholly realized. It is concerned not merely with the things that are seen, but also with the things that are not seen; with the suggestion of new desires and the quickening of new wants. The charity-visitor in the squalid home not only provides food and clothing for the day's necessity, but applies herself to stir the motives of self-help, the need of cleanliness, the hope of opportunity, the impulse of thrift. What is she in all this but an ethical idealist, touching the unconscious capacity for idealism in discouraged lives, and summoning it to vitality and power? This is not sentimentalism supplanting science; it is, on the contrary, science with momentum, works moved by faith, government strengthened by humanity, prudence transfigured by pity. The work of charity, whether in its public or private form, remains halting, intermittent, extravagant, and despondent, until Egoism and Prudentialism are fulfilled in Idealism, and the humblest forms of service are steadied and illuminated by the vision of a world of love.

What is true of these inner social circles of the family and the community becomes even more dramatic in its teaching when one enters the larger circle of modern industrialism. Many persons, though intimately concerned with the conflicts of the business world, are apparently unaware of the real nature of their own social problem. They fancy that it is a purely economic issue, concerned with arrangements of wages or hours or the distribution of profits. The real industrial issue, however, lies in most instances much deeper than these economic adjustments, in the sense of injustice, inhumanity, or wrong. Even when the industrial question is thus recognized as an ethical question, it may still be approached on the lower levels of morality. The employer may satisfy his sense of duty in terms of Egoism. He owns his employed; he is their head and they are his hands. What is his duty but to promote his own business, and suppress the restlessness of his ignorant and ill-advised "help"? The same rudimentary ethics may control the employed. They also may be organized for opposition or revolution. The ethics of industry thus become the ethics of war. What helps one party to the conflict hurts the other. The field of business is a battle-field, where ignorant armies are clashing in the dark. Egoism in business, however, is as self-defeating as in the family or in philanthropy. The more absolutely the employer enforces his authority, the more violent becomes the revolt of the employed. Nietzsche's Master-moralists may count the masses of men as slaves, but the dynasty of the strong is a prophecy of the insurrection of the weak. Despotism is the forerunner of emancipation; industrial feudalism is premonitory of industrial liberty. The same reaction occurs from the egoism of the employed. The more extreme the demands of wage-earners become, the more determined becomes the resistance of the employers. Organization is met by combination; assault by strategy; the massive force of labor by the invisible force of capital. War becomes as ruinous in industry as in politics. A stable business world cannot be built on the ethics of Egoism.

There follows, therefore, in the moralizing of industry, the contribution of Prudentialism. Internecine conflict being recognized as suicidal, there ensues arbitration, conciliation, the balance of expediencies. The two armies of production remain frankly hostile to each other, organizing their forces on a war-footing, and guarding their respective frontiers; but instead of fighting, they negotiate a treaty, or maintain a truce. It is a great step toward industrial peace when reason is thus substituted for force, and passion is given time to cool. Yet Prudentialism in industry, as in politics, does not pretend to settle the issue involved. Though it may prolong peace, it is prepared for war. Precisely as the world-powers build new battleships as a guarantee of peace, so the forces of industry must be strong enough to fight if they would hope to avoid fighting. The same inconclusiveness and the same extravagance which put international politics under a fearful strain reappear in a great proportion of the relations between employers and employed. The class-conscious conflict remains unmitigated. The delicately adjusted balance of rights is likely to be at any moment disturbed. Prudentialism easily reverts to Egoism. The truce of industry may be abruptly broken by war.

Through these successive phases of rudimentary morality emerges by degrees the real Labor Question. It is not, as has often been imagined, a mere struggle of industrial forces for control; it is rather a struggle of industrial idealism for existence. Can there be a practicable substitute for industrial war? Must the forces of economic production be permanently aligned in hostile armies, each with its class-conscious desires, and each restrained from fighting only by diplomacy or by force? Is a Peace-movement practicable in business as it has become practicable among nations? Is the dream of industrial disarmament as remote as the dream of international peace? What is all this but the application of ethical idealism to economic life, the signs of a faith that, even among the brutal and reckless conflicts of industry, the self-realization of each factor must be attained through the service of the organic life? How remote and visionary such a faith may seem to the ordinary business man, overwhelmed by the details and routine of his task! Yet, in the emergence, which may be observed at many points, through the commercialism of the time, of this ideal of industrial unity, the better organization of industrial life must be attained. Each legislative measure which assumes a social responsibility for the defenceless or the weak; each enforcement of sanitation or provision for security; each genuine contribution of an employer or a corporation to the principle of industrial partnership; each alliance of wage-earners for coöperation and mutual aid, — is nothing else than an expression of moral idealism in terms of the business world. From the trader's point of view such enterprises may be regarded as Quixotic and extravagant; but the first evidence of insight and foresight in the administration of business under the conditions of the modern world is the capacity to recognize that stability and efficiency are dependent on unity and peace, and the ingenuity to devise, on terms of mutual self-respect, a working plan of moral idealism. What Harnack has lately said of international peace may be with equal justice said of the peace of industry. "No intelligent man believes in a universal world-state — a Platonopolis; but the promise of 'peace on earth among men of good-will' has already become the watchword of leaders and men of insight."[1]

The Labor-movement, in other words, is not so simple a thing as many men concerned with it suppose. It is not a mere scramble for the spoils of industry, or a mere trial of brute strength between employers and employed. Stupid people will continue to regard it in this stupid way, and will obstruct by their stupidity the creation of a stable business world. The Labor-movement can be understood and effectively promoted by none but idealists. "The future of civilization," a German economist has said, "will chiefly depend on the development in human society of the ethical ideal of justice, — a justice attained not by formal legislation, or considerations of self-interest, but by the recognition and respect in personal conduct of the equal rights of all other persons."[2] The Labor-movement, in other words, is not a scheme or a programme, but — as its title implies — a movement, a stream of tendency, which bears on its surface much scum of self-interest, and many eddies of hesitating Pru-

[1] *Hibbert Journal*, October, 1909, p. 9.
[2] Lexis, "Wesen und Werden der modernen Kultur," *Internat. Wochenschrift*, August 28, 1909.

dentialism; but which, in its main current, is a broadening river of Idealism, seeking its outlet in industrial justice and peace.

Finally, there opens before the student of modern life, beyond these social circles of the family, the community, and the industrial order, the sphere of those larger interests which meet one as a citizen in a modern State. How shall he interpret the political problems which each nation is called to face? How shall he estimate the traits and tendencies of American civilization? What ethical principles can secure national efficiency and peace? At what point has the United States arrived in the evolution of its political ethics? It is, of course, impossible to cover a continent with a single definition, or to discover in the unprecedented diversity of races, colors, and creeds which the American Republic comprehends, a single standard of moral excellence. Yet the amazing capacity for assimilation which this heterogeneous material exhibits has moulded great numbers of people into a similarity of character which may fairly be described as the American type. What is this type which has been thus evolved; and what is the moral problem with which it is now confronted?

The most familiar answer to this question is suggested by the economic prosperity of the country. Its people have become a commercial democracy. Its typical citizen is the successful moneymaker. Its ethics are the ethics of trade. The amazing expansion of its industrial activities has

IDEALISM AND THE SOCIAL QUESTION 159

brought with it a commercial morality, a vulgar materialism, an undisguised worship of Mammon. Is not a rich American described as "a successful man"; and is not any business, if lucrative, described as "a good business"? This estimate of the American character has been expressed by many foreign observers, after brief visits to the country, or superficial study of its affairs. "The Americans," a distinguished German scholar has remarked, "from oldest to youngest hurl themselves into the chase of the dollar. . . . They are a vigorous people, but without substantial culture, without richness of nature, without amiability. It is a land of work, speculation, hurry, gain, or loss. . . . Enthusiasm is rare in the United States, coolness is necessary in order to grow rich. . . . The sight of Niagara suggests to the Yankee nothing but the thought of how much water-power is running to waste."[1] To the same effect is the testimony of a brilliant German novelist, after his journey through the United States. "The daily life of Americans," he says, "has the great drawback of monotony. . . . Life has lost its finer shadings, or what artists call its atmosphere; it seems to be all foreground-painting. The strength of the American is practical, and the ideal is relatively neglected."[2]

It must be frankly admitted that there are many aspects of American life which tend to confirm these judgments. Arrogant commercialism, vulgar

[1] Schmoller, op. cit., I, 157.
[2] von Polenz, "Das Land der Zukunft," 1904, s. 76, 77.

wealth, and speculative recklessness are unquestionably conspicuous features of American life, and may not unreasonably appear to the casual observer its typical traits. The chase of the dollar has been not only exciting, but prodigiously successful. When, however, one enters more intimately into the spirit of the American people, he is met by another trait of national character, which may seem quite inconsistent with the instincts of commercialism, but which is not less typical and effective. It is an inexpugnable and persistent faith in ethical idealism. By one of the most curious coincidences of human history a people, tempted as few nations have been to unbridled materialism and moral levity, still feels in its blood a hereditary strain of moral seriousness. Each movement of the early migrations, which determined the character of the first settlers on the continent, was the consequence of some upheaval of conscience, driving souls before it, as a volcanic upheaval drives a wave across the sea. Religious zeal swept the Jesuit missionaries across the Northern wilderness to the Mississippi; German pietism made the Alleghanies ring with hymns; Moravian missionaries consecrated the soil of Ohio; the Society of Friends gave a State the name of Penn, and a city the name of brotherly love; English Puritanism stamped its tradition on the conscience of New England. Changes in social circumstances may obscure but cannot obliterate these inherited traits. The American people remain strangely susceptible to the appeal of moral idealism. No public question can kindle popular enthusiasm unless it be — or at least appear to be — a moral question, which can be preached as a crusade. No public leader can command the heart of the nation unless he speak — or at least pretend to speak — to the conscience of the nation. Economic prosperity has brought with it, not indolence and satiety, but new expenditures of energy on new enterprises of public service, scientific research, and social reform. Never was there such accumulation of money, yet never such distribution of money for education, philanthropy, and the relief of suffering. Never were wages so high, yet never did wage-earners demand so insistently new resources of liberty and culture.

Here is a more complex type of civilization than a commercial democracy might be expected to produce; a people who are at once acquisitive and generous, hard and soft, shrewd and lavish, commercialists and idealists, creating what an observant Englishman has called a land of contrasts, where the discreditable and the admirable, irreverence and seriousness, cant and patriotism, must be comprehended, like prairie and mountain, fertility and desert, in the total picture of national life. In other words, the United States finds itself now confronted by that crisis in social evolution which, from the point of view of ethical philosophy, is the most interesting and dramatic epoch of national as of personal life, where the forces of Egoism and Prudentialism, which have poured down upon the country as though to submerge it in animalism and materialism, are met by a countercurrent of temper and tradition flowing from the springs of national idealism. Where these two streams meet there must be collision, commotion, danger; and it may be reasonably questioned whether the calmer movement of inherited faith may not be drowned by the turbid torrent of modern commercialism. One truth, however, the theory of ethics and the evidence of history concur in teaching, — that the destiny of a nation — and in this case it may be the destiny of the world — is likely to be determined at this point of moral decision. Many a great nation has been submerged by its own prosperity, and forfeited its place in history through the loss of its moral power. Egypt, Persia, Rome, once the rulers of the world, have become its solemn warnings; while the idealism of Greece and of Judea still satisfies the thirst of the world with its abundant stream. "Where there is no vision," said the Book of Proverbs, "the people perish." It is as profitable a maxim for America as for Palestine. If the American Democracy should crumble and decay like the empires of the past, it would be the same loss of idealism, the same atrophy of moral sensitiveness, which would cause its fall. Can a people, which has been so extraordinarily successful in the conquest of nature, learn to conquer itself? Is the growth of American industrialism to bring with it moral exhaustion, like that of ancient Rome, so that the same epitaph may be written : —

> "Strong was its arm, each thew and bone
> Seem'd puissant and alive —
> But, ah ! its heart, its heart was stone,
> And so it could not thrive ! "[1]

or is it to come to pass that the sagacity and energy which commercialism has developed may create a new type of social idealism, applying these gains to the service of the common good?

Such is the ethical problem which confronts the American Democracy; and it reproduces in the supreme issues of social life the same moral crisis which the institution of the family and the organization of industry have already illustrated. Everywhere the forces of self-interest and expediency contend against the idealist's faith ; and everywhere social stability and progress are determined by the idealist's hope. Not trade, or crops, or ships, or armies, are the guarantees of national security and peace. A nation, like a person, is rich through inheritance of idealism, and prospers through its increase. By faith, said the great epic of the Epistle to the Hebrews, did the elders have witness born to them; by faith they looked for a city which had foundations; yet they received not the promise, "God having provided some better thing for us, that they without us should not be made perfect." It is a

[1] Arnold, "Lyric Poems," 1889, p. 235, "Obermann Once More !"

parable of American life. By faith the fathers went out, not knowing whither they went; and if their sons are to look for a city that has foundations, and expect to secure the better things which the elders could not see, it must be by the same faith in the creative efficiency of national idealism.[1]

[1] As these pages pass through the press, I find their teaching happily confirmed, and indeed anticipated, by the delightful lectures of Professor Jones of Glasgow ("Idealism as a Practical Creed," Glasgow, 1909). His sweep of intellectual horizon, his recognition of poetry as the handmaid of philosophy, and his sense of liberty in loyalty to the ideal, reassure one who follows with less certain steps along the same philosophical road. "Philosophy," teaches Professor Jones, "is an attitude of mind rather than a doctrine. . . . The speculation of the philosopher, the imagination of the poet, and the tumultuous strivings of the man of action blend together." "The call of the modern age" is the call of idealism. "The expansion of the range of ethical responsibility; the greater complexity of the modern State; the deeper implication of the lives of the individual citizens therein; the increase in the variety of its functions, and therefore in its capacity either for mischief or for good; its more democratic character, which subjects it only to its own caprice and with the removal of external restraints makes inner restraint imperative; the irrelevance of the Individualism of the past to its more highly organic character, and the impractical and unethical character of the Socialism of the present — all these things taken together constitute a reason, which is also a necessity, for the more earnest questioning of our ideals of life." (p. 220.)

VI

RELIGION AND THE SOCIAL QUESTION

A final inquiry still confronts the student of the Social Question. As he applies to its interpretation the principles of ethical idealism, is he not, in fact, passing the boundary of ethics, and entering the province of religion? What is this direction of life toward an ideal end, this pull on conduct from the things that are unseen and eternal, this yielding of life to the imperative persuasion of the Perfect, but a witness of the abiding vitality of the religious life? Has not the key of ethics unlocked a more sacred chamber of the spirit than it had seemed designed to open, and do we not enter through this open door the shrine of religious experience and desire? To approach the Social Question by the roads of social science, sociology, economics, and ethics, one must laboriously trudge across vast and often arid plains of experience; but does not religion traverse the same region without hindrance or check as if by the aërial navigation of the spirit? Is not the Social Question another name for practical religion?

There are, it must be admitted, many signs of the times which point to quite an opposite conclusion. On the one hand, there are many devout people who view with scepticism, if not with hostility, this deflecting of religion from its traditional path of worship to these new ways of work, and the exhausting of the instincts of piety in the activities of philanthropy. Religion, they have been taught to believe, means a personal redemption from sin, or a definite allegiance to Christ; and to identify religion with boys' clubs, gymnasiums, and social settlements, seems to them in some degree disloyal to the cause they are pledged to serve. It has been lately suggested that the Christian religion might be defined as " philanthropy, touched and warmed by reverence for Jesus Christ ";[1] but such a definition would seem to many Christians not only grotesquely insufficient, but completely unhistorical; and they would be apprehensive lest, under this definition, philanthropy might become so touching and warm as to displace reverence for Jesus Christ. The very Christ-likeness of philanthropy may excite in a disciple of Christ a pang of regret. Deeds which are legitimately the product of religion seem detached from their spiritual root, as though they owed nothing to religion. They become a substitute for faith rather than an expression of faith; and the very beauty of the flower may seem an affront to religion if the flower bears another name. Is not the religion of deed, they ask, supplanting the religion of creed, and the love of man preoccupying emotions which

[1] *London Spectator*, January 19, 1907.

were once dedicated to the love of God? "We must not," as a recent writer has said, "get the commissary wagon ahead of the colors. The Church can afford no concession with the spirit of the time, if such it be, which regards meat as more than the life, or holds it possible that man can live by bread alone." [1]

On the other hand, a similar apprehension may be observed among those who are most concerned with the Social Question. Religion is often regarded by them with indifference, or even with contempt. A great part of modern social service has become, either consciously or unconsciously, quite dissociated from religion, as though its sanctions were, for the purpose of philanthropy, superfluous or unreal. "Society," an English scholar has said, "has absorbed into its living tissue a large measure of that moral idealism of which the Church once seemed the solitary representative. . . . The Church in her theory has stood aloof from the World and now the World takes deadly revenge by maintaining the position assigned her, and standing aloof from the Church." [2] Organized charity has found the divisions of Christian creeds so obstructive of united effort that it has in large degree secularized itself, and even prohibited its agents from religious propagandism. The same indifference to formal religion marks the methods of labor organizations in all countries. At the hour when religious people

[1] Hayes-Robbins, in *Atlantic Monthly*, July, 1909, p. 99.
[2] Jacks, in *Hibbert Journal*, October, 1906, pp. 8, 17.

meet for worship, unions of hand-workers meet to deliberate on industrial problems and programmes, and do not hesitate to claim that these debates are quite as instructive and uplifting as sermons. To the average hand-worker religion may appear to be occupied with matters too remote from daily living to possess real interest, and the contemplation of eternity may seem to him a luxury reserved for the capitalist class. "My associates," the president of the American Federation of Labor has announced, "have come to look upon the Church and the ministry as the apologists and defenders of the wrong committed against the interests of the people. . . . They use their exalted positions to discourage and discountenance all practical efforts of the toilers to lift themselves out of the slough of despondency and despair."

When one passes from the organization of labor to the organization of revolution, he meets a temper of mind which is not merely neutral, but often frankly hostile to religion. In the formal programmes of scientific socialism religion, it is true, is announced to be a matter of private concern,[1] and Marx himself was indisposed to any frontal attack upon religion, believing that the law of economic determinism would by its own inevitable fulfilment sweep away the illusions of the churches with other products of capitalism. "Man's consciousness changes with every change in the conditions

[1] "Erklärung der Religion zur Privatsache," *Erfurt Programme*, 1891.

of his material existence. . . . The ruling ideas of every age have ever been the ideas of its ruling class. . . . Law, morality, religion, are to him [the proletarian] so many *bourgeois* prejudices, behind which lurk in ambush just as many *bourgeois* interests."[1] "For a society whose economic relations consist in dealing with its products as commodities and values . . . Christianity with its cult of the abstract man, especially in its *bourgeois* development as Protestantism, Deism, etc., is the most appropriate form of religion. . . . The religious reflection of the real world will only then finally vanish when the conditions of practical work-a-day life establish rational relations with man and with nature." "It is much easier to find by analysis the earthly kernel of the misty creations of religion than, conversely, to develop from the actual relations of life its religious forms. The latter is the only method of materialism, and therefore the scientific method."[2] "The value [of linen] is shown by its equality with the coat, as the sheep's nature of a Christian is shown by his resemblance to the Lamb of God."[3] The note of teaching thus struck by Marx is repeated by many of his disciples in less controlled and more strident tones. Religion, wrote Bebel, "will not be abolished, or God dethroned. . . . Without attack of force or sup-

[1] Marx and Engels, "Manifesto of the Communist Party," Engl. tr., 1898, pp. 39, 40, 28.
[2] Marx, "Das Kapital," 2te Aufl., 1872, I, s. 56, 57, 386.
[3] Marx, op. cit. I, s. 27.

pression of opinion of any kind, religion will of itself vanish. It is the transcendent reflection of the existing social order. . . . Morality and Ethics have nothing to do with religion; simpletons and hypocrites maintain the contrary."[1] "What, indeed, is agnosticism," said Engels, "but . . . 'shamefaced' materialism? . . . Tradition is a great retarding force, is the *vis inertiæ* of history, but, being merely passive, is sure to be broken down; and thus religion will be no lasting safeguard to capitalist society."[2] "God, as Laplace said, is an hypothesis of which exact science has no need. . . . Science and religion are in inverse ratio to each other; the one diminishes and grows weaker in the same proportion that the other increases and grows stronger in its struggle against the unknown."[3] "Christian Socialism," said Marx and Engels, "is but the Holy Water with which the priest consecrates the heart-burnings of the aristocrat."[4] Thus, the social revolutionists concur with the theological reactionists in their distrust of an intimacy between religion and the Social Question. To the one group social amelioration appears a meagre substitute for religion; to the other group it creates a new religion, with the same appeal to brother-

---

[1] Op. cit., s. 313, 314, 315.

[2] "Socialism Utopian and Scientific," tr. Aveling, 1892, pp. xiv, xxxvii.

[3] Ferri, "Socialism and Modern Science," tr. La Monte, 1904, pp. 60, 61.

[4] Op. cit., 1898, p. 46.

hood and sacrifice which traditional religion has made. "Socialism," Liebknecht is reported to have said, "is at once a science and a religion; in its appeal to the feeling and the conscience it has the entire force of Christianity; in its appeal to the mind it has all the strength of science." [1]

If, then, the gulf between religion and the Social Question, viewed from either side, appears so wide, and apprehension on the one hand is confronted by indifference on the other, must it be inferred that religion has lost its hold upon the modern mind? On the contrary, such a conclusion fails to recognize either the nature of the Social Question or the nature of the religious life. If religion represented nothing but ecclesiastical machinery and dogmatic opinions, and if the Social Question represented nothing but a programme for the distribution of industrial profits, then they would certainly occupy regions so remote from each other that loyalty to one might mean betrayal of the other. There is little in common between debates on the orders of clergy or the condition of sinners after death and discussions of a wage-scale or an eight-hour day. But if, on the other hand, both religion and the Social Question are primarily concerned with life, conduct, duty, feeling, hope; if both are interpretations of experience in the world that now is, — then it is not only needless, but it is impossible, to hold them asunder. The religion

[1] Cited in Kaufmann, "Socialism and Modern Thought," 1895, p. ix.

which is fit for the present age must be a social religion; the Social Question which the present age has to answer must be a religious question; and both for religion and the Social Question the most imminent peril of contemporary thought is the peril of provincialism, — the dealing with great truths as though they were small and shut-in experiences, set in a corner of life as the special concern of a single class. If either religion or the Social Question has any meaning for the world, it is a universal meaning; not as though they were evanescent eddies in the stream of time, but as the sweep of its main current between the banks of successive ages to the sea of human destiny. If, then, there is this similarity of nature and intention, how may the appearance of remoteness and isolation be removed, and the affinities of religion and the Social Question be disclosed? What are the marks of religion as a social force, and what are the marks of the Social Question as a religious fact?

In the first place, it should be noticed, alike by teachers of religion and by preachers of social righteousness, that both religion and the Social Question have a singular similarity in practical consequences which suggests a similarity in origin. The same ideals and aspirations, which have been in other generations the peculiar property of religion, have in this generation reappeared in forms of the Social Question. Emotions which once uttered themselves in prayer, conversion, and oral pledges, are now uttering themselves in philanthropy, social service, and industrial reform. The finding of life in losing it, the service which is perfect freedom, self-realization in self-sacrifice, — these familiar paradoxes of the religious life are now not less familiar as social paradoxes. Religion uses the language of service not less than that of faith. Each religious organization, if it would justify its existence, adds to its machinery of worship a further machinery of work. It accepts the ancient test of discipleship, "By their fruits ye shall know them"; it condemns as the cardinal sin of religion the sin of Cain, "Am I my brother's keeper"; it holds as the most precious words of Jesus his self-dedication to human service, "For their sakes I sanctify myself."

Shall one say, then, that this identity of operations indicates that religion is displaced by the new social spirit, or is it more reasonable to conclude that the Social Question is but a new channel through which flows the unexhausted stream of the religious life? Even though the social movement is not the main highway of the religious life, may it not be the way which lies most immediately before the mind of the present age, and which indicates that step in God's education of the human race which this generation is called by Him to take? There are many paths by which the life of man may reach the life of God; but may one not become so accustomed by tradition and training to one of these paths that he fails to see another way which lies directly before his feet? When the Pharisees were confronted by the teaching of Jesus, they applied to it their preconception of what it should be, rather than their appreciation of what it was; and in failing to meet their preconceived test, it failed to command their loyalty. It was the same even with certain disciples, when Jesus was discovered not to be what they had fancied he would be. He "drew near," it is written, "and went with them. But their eyes were holden that they should not know him."[1] They were so preoccupied in thinking that this should have been he who was to redeem Israel, that they did not recognize the Messiah of the human soul walking by their side. And what self-reproach could be more keen than this, — to meet the same spirit of self-effacing service walking, as on the path to Emmaus, along the dusty track of the Social Question, and to have one's eyes holden, even though one's heart burned within him on the way?

A young man, for example, comes one day to his teacher, and with intense feeling asks, "Can you tell me of a Boys' Club where I might be of use?" "Why, then," inquires the older man, "do you care to undertake this social service in the middle of your busy winter?" "Because," answers the youth, "my life seems empty and tempted, until I do something for somebody else." It was a boyish answer, made in the language of his own age. The way of consecration, if it was to be found by him at

[1] Luke xxiv. 16.

all, must be discovered along the path of the Social Question. The only natural utterance for his restless heart was the pledge of service. But was not this call of the social conscience a summons from the same spiritual impulses which, under the conditions of earlier generations, would have led that youth to an oral confession of sin or an experience of conversion? Was it not in a new dialect the ancient cry of Augustine, "My heart is restless, until it finds rest in Thee!"? In other words, must not religion use the language which is natural to each successive age, and must not teachers of religion be quick to recognize the accents of the spirit, even though the speech be in an unfamiliar tongue? One might regret that such a youth had not been trained to believe that this call to sanctify himself for others' sakes was a call from God; yet the first duty of any judicious counsellor would be, none the less, to open the door at which the boy was knocking, and bid him follow the path which lay before his feet. The first test of a saving faith must be, not orthodoxy, but reality; not conformity, but efficiency; and the gravest indictment which could be brought against the religious teaching of any age would be, not that it failed to express the whole gospel, but that it failed to hear the real voice of the soul, or to see the way which a life had to go. Such were the deafness and blindness of those who in the days of Jesus Christ could not receive his new and surprising message, and to whom he applied the withering irony of Isaiah: "This people's heart is waxed gross, and their ears are dull of hearing, and their eyes they have closed; lest at any time they should see with their eyes, and hear with their ears, and understand with their heart, and should be converted and I should heal them."[1]

These intimations of a common origin are, then, not without importance. If a tree is to be known by its fruits, then the roots of religion and of social service would seem to be of the same stock. The fruits of the latter may not be as ripe and varied as those of the former, but their similarity in flavor and form suggests that the Social Question may be a graft from the religious life. Is there, however, one now goes on to ask, in addition to this likeness of operations, evidence of a real kinship, which stamps the Social Question with a definitely religious character and aim? To answer this question one must pause to inquire what is the nature of religion, and what is the organ of expression which it most naturally employs? And here there meet one the various philosophies of religion, which interpret in different ways the nature of the religious life. Is religious experience primarily a form of thought, or a movement of emotion, or a decision of the will? Are we in religion primarily rationalists, or mystics, or ethical idealists? Is religion fundamentally a doctrine, or a feeling, or a resolve?

The history of the philosophy of religion has, for the most part, considered the first two of these

[1] Matt. xiii. 15; Is. vi. 9.

definitions. Either, as with Hegel, the reason has appeared the medium of the Eternal; or, as with Schleiermacher, the feelings have appeared to offer a channel of communion, deeper and more direct than the reason can provide. This issue between Rationalism and Mysticism, the religion of thought and the religion of emotion, has seemed the *crux* of the philosophy of religion, as though between these two alternatives the devout life must choose. Is there not, however, a third way of communion between the soul and the Eternal; a path which leads from morality to faith; a way in which the will becomes a guide; a road not reserved either for scholars or for saints, but accessible to that great multitude of plain people whose religion consists in little more than the simple desire to do their duty? This is the path to the heights of certitude which was first explored by Kant, and has now been made familiar by Fichte and by Martineau. It leads from decision to insight; from duty to vision; from fidelity to faith; from loyalty to piety; from obedience to knowledge. "With surprising clearness," said Fichte,[1] "does this thought, which was hitherto veiled in obscurity, now reveal itself to my soul; the thought that my will, merely as such and through itself, shall have results. It has results, because it is immediately and infallibly perceived by another Will to which it is related, which is its own accomplishment and the only living principle of the

[1] "Popular Works," tr. Smith, 4th ed., 1889, I, p. 457, from the "Vocation of Man."

spiritual world. . . . The voice of conscience in my soul which teaches me in every situation of life what I have there to do, is the channel through which again His influence descends upon me." "If," said Martineau [1] to the same purpose, "the moral consciousness be in very truth a communion between the Divine and the human mind, . . . a great redemption comes, and . . . converts the life of Duty into the life of Love. . . . The rule of right, the symmetries of character, the requirements of perfection, are no provincialisms of this planet; they are known among the stars." "The vocation and dignity of man," taught Paulsen,[2] "is not ultimately rooted in knowledge, but in the volitional side of his nature. Here also lie the deepest roots of our being; in conscience, in the consciousness of the moral law, we become aware of our real essence. We possess the immediate certainty that we belong . . . in a moral world-order, of which the natural order is but an external reflection. One's view of the world receives its most powerful and decided impetus, not from the understanding, but from the volitional side, from the practical reason."

Frederic Robertson, interpreting his teacher Fichte, has translated these academic phrases into the language of life. "Obedience," he says, in one of his greatest sermons, "is the organ of spiritual

---

[1] "A Study of Religion," 1888, I, pp. 27, 28.

[2] "Introduction to Philosophy," tr. Thilly, 2d Amer. ed., 1906, pp. 419, 420, 321.

knowledge. In every department of knowledge there is an appropriate 'organ,' or instrument for discovery of its specific truth. . . . Obedience is the sole organ by which we gain a knowledge of that which cannot be seen or felt. . . . By doing God's will we recognize what He is."[1] The philosophy of religion, thus approached, becomes the fulfilment of that ethical idealism whose emergence in the moral process has been already described. To follow the line of duty-doing, as it runs through Egoism and Prudentialism to Idealism, is to enter at last the circle of religion. To prolong the radius of goodness is to penetrate the sphere of faith. The outer edge of ethics is the inner margin of religion. "The law of duty," as Sabatier has said, "shares in the objectivity of cosmic laws themselves."[2]

It must not be inferred from these teachings that the different ways, thus described, of approach to the religious life are to be regarded as fixed alternatives, to one of which alone the spiritual life must conform. On the contrary, the paths of thought and feeling and will repeatedly meet and cross each other, like tracks upon a hillside, where the climber may pass from one to another to ease or quicken his ascent. The most hardened rationalist is never safe from the inrush of emotion;

---

[1] "Sermons," II, 137. Cf. also the citations in Peabody, "Jesus Christ and the Christian Character," 1906, pp. 96, 244 ff.

[2] "Religions of Authority and the Religion of the Spirit," 1904, p. 350.

and the most passive mystic cannot altogether escape the call of the will. It was a mystic of the seventeenth century who wrote of his religious experience: "My mind was not at rest, because nothing was acted (*i.e.* done), and thoughts ran in me that words and writings were all nothing and must die; for action is the life of all, and if thou dost not act, thou dost nothing."[1]

It is still further evident that these different ways to faith offer themselves with varying degrees of accessibility in different periods of religious history. At one time the high-road of doctrinal authority seems the way which all men must take; yet suddenly, as in the Mediæval Church, before the reformation of doctrine is attempted, certain devout souls strike off, as it were, from the main road of ecclesiasticism into the by-path of mysticism, and find a delightful prospect on this unfamiliar track. At another period the religion of feeling seems to have exhausted itself, like a path which comes to an end in the woods, and an age dominated by practical motives takes up its march along the plain way of doing good.

It may perhaps be maintained, still further, that these various avenues to religious insight offer themselves with varying persuasion at different periods of personal experience, and meet one in succession as his own life proceeds. The religion of youth is not infrequently a religion of rationalism. The

[1] Winstanley, cited by Jones, "Studies in Mystical Religion," 1909, II, p. 499.

intellectual life is just starting on its long journey, and sets out with the exhilaration and freshness of the morning. Eternal truth seems waiting to be overtaken just beyond the first turn of the road. "Philosophy is the helmsman of life," repeats the young scholar as he wins his first academic prize; and the philosophy which he has for the moment happened to appropriate takes the helm of his spiritual destiny. As youth passes into manhood, however, a new world of spiritual experiences opens before the mature life, and through that world of love and hope, of desire and sacrifice, a new way seems to lead to peace. It is the mystic's path of exalted and illuminated emotion. Instead of self-assertion there is self-surrender, and, through it, self-discovery. Instead of the pride of freedom there is the humility of dependence. What the youthful rationalist had scorned as emotionalism, the riper mystic welcomes as vision. Finally, it may happen that, as intellectual limitations become more clearly recognized, and as emotional agitations subside, the religion of maturity may turn, with patience yet with assurance, to the less ambitious path which leads, not over the heights of intellectual certainty, nor through the picturesque valleys of mysticism, but along the dusty plain of common duty-doing. The way of reason may seem too steep, and the way of feeling too tortuous; but straight before one's feet, in the business of daily life, lies the plain road of moral idealism; and as the will trudges along this unromantic road it finds the way growing steadily more inviting and ascending, until the paths of the reason and of the emotions join the prosaic way of obligation, and lead one to the heights. Obedience proves to be the organ of spiritual knowledge; doing the will has fulfilled itself in the knowledge of the doctrine. The promise has been verified: "Seek first the Kingdom of God and his righteousness; and all these things shall be added unto you."[1]

Nothing, then, could be more unlike real experience than a philosophy of religion which should bar all but one of these ways of the spirit. They are all open ways; and each offers itself with special solicitation to a special mood, or need, or phase of life or history. Each is not only a legitimate, but an inevitable choice. To obstruct the free movement of thought toward the Eternal, either by the proof of its futility or by the condemnation of its doubts, is as vain as to prohibit the movement of the tides. Rationalism is the rising tide of the reason. The mind of man is lifted by cosmic necessity toward the thought of God. Not less accessible is the way of mysticism. Throughout the history of religion this path has been traversed and illuminated by a great company of witnesses, testifying to their companionship with the Eternal. It must be admitted, however, that the circumstances of the present age make the ways of rationalism and of mysticism to many minds

[1] Matt. vi. 33.

difficult to follow. The proofs of God, ontological or teleological, which satisfied Anselm or Paley, fail to convince the scientific mind; the emotional response, which greeted Whitefield or Fox, is checked by more complex experience. The age of the Social Question has made many people less confident in their metaphysics, and less scrutinizing of their own souls. To such a time, then, and to people primarily concerned with action, efficiency, and service, there offers itself, as though designed for immediate use, the way to God which leads through the dedication of the will. Many mysteries of truth may be, for the moment, undisclosed; many exalted experiences of religious feeling may seem visionary and unrealizable; but the call to social duty, the imperative of social idealism, the finding of life in losing it, the happiness of living not to be ministered unto but to minister, — these persuasions issue from the very nature of the modern world and the very instincts of the modern mind; and if a way to religious confidence is to be found at all, it is likely to be found, not by rejecting the path which lies before one and re-opening ways that lead from other times and other needs, but in setting out along the open road, where the will leads and the reason and feelings follow.

It may be urged that this is but to take up the path of philosophy now so warmly defended and condemned under the name of Pragmatism; that the supremacy of the will is but another name for empiricism, experimentalism, probabilism, the confession of bankruptcy for the faith of idealism. Quite another way, however, from this is that which leads toward the religious life. It does not begin by wishing and end by guessing; it begins by doing and ends in knowing. Pragmatism has done great service to modern thought by indicating the importance of the will in the direction of life; but it has failed to observe the process of experience which the dedication of the will initiates. The will is, in fact, a medium of insight, and the dedication of the will to spiritual ends is a path to spiritual certainty. Just as one comes to believe in love by loving, and in hope by hoping, so the spiritual order of the world comes into view as one sets the will to serve the world. Self-forgetting philanthropy is the best remedy for religious doubt. Not the will to believe, but the will to help, is the open path to insight and vision. The natural corollary to self-scrutiny is pessimism; the more one urges his will to believe, the less he may find to believe in. The world that centres in one's own will must soon seem an empty world. Rational optimism, on the other hand, is the normal product of the socialized will, the will to help. The world becomes interesting and beautiful as one participates in its redemption. The dedication of the will leads, not to self-deception, but to self-discovery. The life of service is not a substitute for reality, but an assurance of reality. Such would be the glad and humble testimony of many lives, who have heard the call of the present age and answered it with the dedication of their wills. They have gone out, not knowing whither they went; and have been led along the path of self-forgetting service to a peace and hope which they had not expected to attain. They have done, not their own wills, but the will of Him that sent them; and have accomplished that task which He has given them to do.

Nor is this modern experience without the most trustworthy historical verification; for when one turns back to the teaching of Jesus Christ, he finds no note of that teaching more characteristic than this summons to the will. Jesus was not a psychologist, academically discriminating between the functions of the spirit; but he certainly had an extraordinary gift for interpreting human lives to themselves. The secrets of many hearts, it was prophesied of him, should be revealed; and this disclosure to many hearts of the secret springs of their own conduct and faith gave to many hearers their first sense of happy surprise as they listened to his message. Standing, then, before the threefold mystery of the mind and heart and will, to what spiritual capacity does Jesus turn for the first expression of discipleship? What way to faith does he bid his followers go? The answer to this question is written on every page of the Gospels. Great disclosures of truth were made by him to the reason, and he might be remembered among the world's philosophers if he had not earned a higher title. Great exaltations of emotion marked the crises of his career, at Cæsarea Philippi and Gethsemane, and justify his followers in claiming the right to a direct and immediate communion with their God. Neither rationalism nor mysticism, however, represents the habitual attitude of his mind, or his habitual way of instruction and persuasion. The primary teaching of Jesus Christ was to the will. His first demand of those who would be his disciples was neither theological accuracy nor mystic ecstasy, but practical obedience and moral decision. "Follow me; Take up thy cross and follow; Seek first the Kingdom of God and his righteousness; If any man willeth to do the will he shall know of the doctrine" — these are the great commands which go echoing through the Gospels. "I am the way," he says with a reiterated emphasis which gave to the Christian religion itself the title of the "Way." This dedication of the will is not the whole of the religion of Jesus; it is perhaps not the best of that religion; but it is unquestionably the beginning of it. Wonderful revelations of truth may be seen along that road of discipleship; and high moments of rapture may be attained; but the way to a consistent Christian rationalism and an undisquieted Christian mysticism lies up the steep path of moral obedience and self-forgetting service, which the disciple of Jesus is bidden, even with stumbling or bleeding feet, to climb.

Shall we then conclude that Jesus was a teacher

of ethics rather than a revealer of religion? On the contrary, it is precisely because he was the first that he became the second. It is along the way of human service that the disciple of Jesus reaches the height of religious vision. And here is precisely where great numbers of persons, who propose to be disciples of Jesus, make their fundamental mistake. They have thought they could begin by applying to the subject their minds or their hearts, without, first of all, enlisting their wills. They have kept their religion in one compartment of experience, where it commends itself to the reason or to the feelings, but where it does not seriously affect their conduct. "Things have come to a pretty pass," Lord Melbourne is reported to have said after hearing an evangelical sermon, "when religion is allowed to invade the sphere of private life."[1] The teaching of Jesus proposes nothing less than this disturbing invasion of private life. It tolerates no schism between the mind and the will, no double standard of living, no theological bimetallism. The silver of ethics and the gold of religion are interchangeable mediums of spiritual exchange. Ethics is the fractional currency of the unit of value, and as it accrues becomes religion. Thus, it is difficult at many points of the Gospels to say whether the teaching is ethical or religious. The Sermon on the Mount is a discourse on ethics; the Beatitudes are moral precepts; yet at each step in the Sermon, and at the close of each

[1] "Collections and Recollections," 1903, p. 58.

Beatitude, the Teacher, as it were, points out beyond the path of conduct the vision of faith to which it leads. The poor in spirit and pure in heart are to be blessed, but their blessing is in inheriting God's Kingdom and in seeing God as He is. Thus the contemporary and the Eternal, moral obedience and spiritual vision, ethical idealism and rational Theism, the service of man and the vision of God, make — in the teaching of Jesus — one continuous process, beginning in the dedication of the will and ending in conscious communion with the Eternal. If any man willeth to do the will, he shall know of the doctrine.

If, then, among many ways to the religious life there is one which leads through moral obedience to spiritual assurance; if the teaching of Jesus and the teaching of modern philosophy concur in their initial appeal to the will; then, with a new sense of confidence and appreciation, one may recall once more the nature of the Social Question. It has already been recognized as a sign, not merely of commercial self-seeking or economic adjustment, but of the social conscience uttering itself in the language of the present age; it accompanies not declining prosperity but advancing desires; it meets a people, not on their way down, but on their way up; it is the attempt of ethical idealism to find a place for itself among the problems and conflicts of the modern world. If this is the Social Question; if it represents on the largest scale a movement of moral idealism; does it not naturally lead to an end beyond itself and, however unreligious and unsanctified many of its manifestations may appear to be, does it not prophesy a renaissance of practical religion? The theologians of the early church observed in the circumstances of the world before the coming of Christ an unconscious preparation for its welcome, a *"Præparatio Evangelica"* which predisposed expectant minds to the new faith. Is it not possible that the Social Question, which seems to divert many minds from the ancient ways of faith, may predispose them to a new faith in the efficiency of moral idealism, and become a *Præparatio Evangelica* of the twentieth century?

Unconscious of this religious office much of the social agitation of the time certainly is, and many of those concerned with its philanthropic or industrial changes may even protest against this insinuation of a religious aim. Yet this unconscious coöperation with God, or even this denial of it, does not abolish the fact of such a coöperation. Many a ploughman bending over his furrow lifts his eyes but seldom to the sun, which none the less persuades his crop; many a sailor takes little thought of the laws which govern the winds; and with the same unconsciousness many a servant of social needs goes his way with hesitating steps and downcast eyes, as though his life were all routine and drudgery; while none the less, as he trudges along his furrow, he is coöperating with the Sun of Righteousness, or as he navigates the troubled sea of modern life he is running down the trade wind of universal law.

What a strange scene the modern world thus presents, of theoretical indifference and of practical loyalty; of people who think themselves without religion and yet daily testify to the motives of religion! Never were so many minds repelled by the technicalities of religion; yet never were there so many people of whom the great words could be spoken: "Not every one that saith unto me, Lord, Lord, . . . but he that doeth the will of my Father"; never so many who might ask in surprise: "When saw we thee an hungred, and fed thee, or . . . a stranger, and took thee in?" and are fit to receive the answer: "Inasmuch as ye have done it unto these, . . . ye have done it unto me";[1] never so many unconscious Christians, willing to do the will, but neither knowing nor caring to know the doctrine: —

> "Sweet souls, without reproach or blot,
> Who do Thy work and know it not."

At such a time, what is the task of teachers of religion but to clarify and interpret these impulses of service, to indicate their religious implications, and to present the religious life, not as an alternative to social duty, but as its natural and logical fulfilment. What, in a word, is this world-wide and compelling summons to the creation of a

[1] Matt. vii. 21; xxv. 37, 40.

better world but the premonition of a revival of faith in man as the instrument, and faith in the world as the object, of redemption? Here is no abandonment of religion, or substitute for religion, but a way — not yet wholly clear, but not impassable — along which the life of the present age may reach a religion appropriate to its own needs. It is perhaps not the most direct way, but it is at least not without the approval of modern philosophy, or without the commendation of Jesus Christ, and for many persons under the conditions of the present age the way most immediately open; and it is not so important in the ascent of faith what way one should take, as it is to start from the point where one finds himself, and not stop till the summit is won.

Such seems to be the relation of the Social Question to the religious life. The two are not competitors or alternatives, but successive experiences, logical steps in the education of the human race. And if this conclusion is legitimate, there follow from it two practical consequences which are of the utmost significance, alike to social service and to religious faith. The first may be described as the spiritualization of the Social Question, and the second may be described as the socialization of the religious life.

What, on the one hand, is the most immediate peril which threatens the Social Question? It is, as has been more than once observed, the peril of a practical materialism; the interpretation of a great human movement in terms of machinery; the expectation that a change in economic methods will of itself produce a change of the human heart. And what, to state the case from the other side, is the chief source of hope and courage in the movement of social service? It is the discovery, which many minds at many points of this great adventure are now making, that beneath the forms of economic change there is proceeding a spiritual enterprise which the present age is called to undertake.

A charity-visitor, for example, enlists in the service of relief, and the problems which confront her — of wages, housing, idleness, food, and drink — seem wholly concerned with economic conditions and material wants. The squalid facts of her task may almost extinguish its spiritual significance, as a flame flickers and dies where the atmosphere is foul. "What room is there," she may ask, "for ethical idealism among these sordid and commercial needs?" "Give me the luxuries of life," the historian, Motley, humorously said, "and I can dispense with its necessities"; and it may well seem to this servant of the poor that philosophy and religion are offering her the luxuries of life, while the necessities of existence are still unsupplied. Must she not abandon her idealism and apply herself to the terribly concrete conditions of her immediate work? On the contrary, her philosophy of charity is essential to her efficiency and courage in the practice of relief. Nothing can redeem the work of charity from dulness and despondency except the capacity for spiritual vision. Let the agent of relief forget her idealism, and she becomes a social mechanic, an official, a statistician, and is on the highroad to discouragement, perfunctoriness, and despair. The mechanism of her task can be endured only as she discerns the meaning of her task. Her philosophy is not a luxury, but a necessity. She is patient with the real because she beholds the ideal. The dull and unresponsive life before her becomes a symbol of her faith, and is transfigured by her idealism into interest, picturesqueness, and sanctity. Her social service has passed the limits of duty and entered the region of privilege. She walks by faith, not by sight; and her faith saves both her and her work from condescension, impatience, and hopelessness. Sir Launfal, seeking the Holy Grail, passed the leper at his own door; but, returning from the distant quest, found the ideal he had sought revealed to him in the duty he had ignored: —

> "And the leper no longer crouched at his side,
> But stood before him glorified,
> Shining and tall and fair and straight
> As the pillar that stood by the Beautiful Gate."

The same story may be told in the language of the industrial world; of many an employer, whose way of business promotes justice, fraternalism, and peace; and of many an employed, whose fidelity and efficiency are such as no wage-system can buy. These men may fancy themselves far from any contact with the religious life; they may listen but languidly to the preachers of other worldliness; they may even conceive of the Christian ministry as a useless caste, and of the Christian Church as a capitalist-club. They are too busy to be pious and too worldly to be saints. And yet, if the Christian character is to have any place in modern life, it must be precisely where these men are set, in the heat of the world's work and under the load of the world's care; and the worst of disasters, alike for religion and for business, is to separate the one from the other. When Jesus looked about him for the habit of life which he desired to commend, he found it most conspicuously in those people who were doing, as it should be done, the common work of the business world. The investor with his talents, the porter at the gate, the farmer in the field, the merchant with his pearls, the woman at her house-work, — how common and worldly, how far from the religion of the Scribes and Pharisees were these types of holiness! Yet of these commonplace people, who had thus spiritualized their Social Question, so that their daily business could meet the test of Christ, he said: The kingdom of heaven is like these. It is the same to-day. Each invention or enterprise which lifts the industrial burden or promotes industrial efficiency; each character forged in the fire of business temptation; each movement of industrial justice, brotherhood, partnership, or peace, is nothing less than the new language in which the men of the present age are uttering their great confession, "We are laborers together with God."

Laurence Oliphant once said that the greatest need of modern England was a spiritually-minded man of the world,—a man, that is to say, who could be in the world, yet not subdued to that he worked in, and who found it not impossible to do the world's work with a spiritual mind. He is like a potter, sitting before the clay which it is his task to mould. He does not wash his hands of it because it soils him, or dabble in it like a little boy for the sake of getting dirty; but he takes it, just as it is, and shapes it into the forms of use or beauty which are possible under the limits of the clay. Precisely such material is the modern business world, and the spiritually-minded man of the world does not dabble in it, or run away from it, but moulds it to the use and beauty to which, just as it is, it may be applied. No harder test was ever offered to the religious life than this demand that it shall adapt itself to the material conditions of an industrial democracy. It must be shaped out of the common clay of commercial conditions and hardened in the fire of industrial temptation. It is called to spiritualize the Social Question, and to make it an instrument of rational and consistent faith. It uses the coarse material of modern life to teach, as Dante said, "How man eternalizes himself."

And if it is the part of religion to spiritualize the Social Question, so, on the other hand, the Social

Question is called to socialize the religious life. The religion of the individual, it is true, remains the permanent centre of spiritual experience. No organization or authority can supplant the right to immediate communion of the individual soul with the living God. The religious life is most directly transmitted by the contagion of the spirit, the communicative power of consecrated souls. Nothing that may happen to religion can convert it into a sociological or economic scheme, which substitutes a change in social conditions for a change in human hearts. Socialism may be religious, but religion is not socialism. "The kingdom of God is within you."

To hold fast to this central thought of personal religion is not, however, to desocialize religion. The religion of the individual is not the religion of individualism. The one makes the person the beginning of the religious process; the other makes him the end of it. Individual religion is the most powerful of social dynamics; individualistic religion, on the other hand, is unapplied power, like an engine which has its proper fuel, but is unattached to moving wheels. The difference is not one of origin or power, but of the transmission of energy. No age can safely subordinate the religion of the individual; yet nothing is more obvious than the fact that the present age has completely outgrown the religion of individualism. The age of the Social Question involves the socialization of the religious life. It is no longer possible to think of religion as a personal possession, or security, or joy; for the mind of the time turns inevitably to the further question of utilization, applicability, and service. Thus the centre of religious experience remains where it always has been, but the radius of religious experience is enormously expanded, toward the ever widening circle of social obligations, hopes, and dreams.

This extension of the sphere of religion is, in fact, occurring in every human interest and aim. The religion of individualism is but sharing the fate of the economics and the politics of individualism. Precisely as the modern miracles of intercommunication have transformed the world into an organism where the progress or decadence of one nation is felt, like pain at the extremities of a body, at the remotest parts; precisely as a new economics and a new politics have issued from this new thought of the unity of the world, — so the circle of religious experience has widened from the problem of personal redemption to the problem of a world to be redeemed; and the individual, instead of being called to save his soul from a lost world, is called to set his soul to save the world. The religion of the twentieth century must contemplate the world, not as a chaos of competing atoms, but as an organic and indivisible whole. It must socialize its hopes, and save people, not singly but together, the poor with the prosperous, the employed with the employer, the Oriental with the Occidental, the Black with the White.

The age of the Social Question has thus brought with it a new extension of the province of the Church; a new conception of Foreign Missions; and a new definition of the Christian Ministry. The Church becomes not so much an association of saints as an association of saviours, not so much a witness of redemption as an instrument of redemption, not so much an ark of refuge as a missionary ship. It is the great company of those who have heard the original call of Jesus, when he "came into Galilee preaching the gospel of the kingdom of God"; and who apply to the service of that kingdom the great law of his own life, "For their sakes I sanctify myself."

Such an organization of redemption acquires a new hope in its missionary work. It was said a generation ago that the abandonment of Calvinism had "cut the nerve of missions," and it is unquestionably true that as the conception of a lost world and a saved remnant has declined, one missionary motive of tremendous solemnity has disappeared. The deepest incision into this nerve of missions has been made, however, not by theological science, but by social science. The new knowledge of the Eastern world promoted by the intercommunication of scholarship, and the profound impressiveness of Oriental civilization, literature, and religion, have made the earlier distinction of saved and lost, privileged and outcast, as preposterous as it was blasphemous, and have led the Church to recall those great affinities of the spirit which the first

Christian missionary announced: He "hath made of one blood all nations of men for to dwell on the face of the earth, . . . that they should seek the Lord, if haply they might feel after him, and find him, though he be not far from every one of us."[1] What is this new consciousness of the unity of the world but a fresh summons to missionary service? To be convinced that the destinies of the nations are one; that the ends of the earth are bound together in mutual dependence; that there are lessons to learn as well as to teach, when Occidental energy touches Oriental contemplation; to find in unfamiliar faiths, not gross darkness, but fundamental truths which may be brought to light; to discover much to build on instead of everything to overthrow; to approach alien faiths not to destroy but to fulfil, — such is the sympathy and hope of which the new missionary spirit is full. The nerve of missions which was cut was a diseased nerve; and the missionary system is healthier for the operation. The socialization of religion is the seed of a new missionary harvest.

The same conception of religion becomes even more effective when applied to the profession of the ministry. It is commonly said that this sacred calling no longer appeals to modern minds, and that the future of religion is imperilled by the lack of men to serve her; and the statistics of theological education seem to confirm this opinion, and to encourage this despondency. If, however, the

[1] Acts xvii. 26, 27.

world with all its needs and hopes is the object of redemption; if the province of religion comprehends the entire range of social amelioration; then the calling of the minister, instead of being stranded on the shores of the present time, finds itself in the very centre of the current of the age, where it feels most immediately the volume and velocity of its flow. Priests there must still be who shall instruct and comfort individual souls; and prophets who shall inspire and warn the congregations of worshippers; but must it be admitted that the ministry is wholly a talking profession, or may it reckon among its members all that great company who come not to be ministered unto, but to minister? Did not Jesus Christ, when citing Scripture to explain his mission, open the Book and find the place where it was written: "The Spirit of the Lord God is upon me, because he hath anointed me to preach the gospel to the poor; . . . and recovering of sight to the blind, to set at liberty them that are bruised."[1] He was a preacher of good tidings to the poor, but was he less a minister when serving the blind and the bruised? Was John Wesley a minister as he preached in the fields, and not John Howard as he served in the prisons? Was Channing in the pulpit a minister, and not Samuel Howe, among the idiots and the blind? The fact is that the world is confronted not so much by an unfortunate decline of the ministry as by an unrecognized expansion of it. The socialization of

[1] Luke iv. 18.

religion has recruited the profession with new allies, and has given a right to new courage among those already in its ranks. Not priests and preachers only, with their still indispensable functions of religious leadership, but the great company of self-effacing servants of the world's needs, who in their various ways are bringing in the acceptable year of the Lord, have chosen for themselves, though so often unaware of their choice, the vocation of the ministry, and should be counted in the statistical records of the profession. When a young man, as now so frequently happens, deliberates whether he shall enter the ministry or enlist in the calling of social service, he is, in fact, not choosing between two professions, but between two departments of the same profession, in each of which the same motives are essential to efficiency. It is not less important that social service should be recognized as a religious work than it is that religious service should be recognized as a social work; and to draw a line between the two is to rob religion of its reality and social service of its sacredness.

The Church of the Middle Ages, whatever may have been its defects, appreciated this comprehensiveness of the religious life, which Protestantism has in large part ignored. The entire civilization of that earlier time was included within the province of the Church. The sacred possessed the secular. Not priests and monks alone were serving the supreme cause; but lay-brothers and nursing-sisters, artists and scholars, the peasant ploughing the fields of the monastery and the scullion washing the utensils of the kitchen, — all these were consciously coöperating in the work of the Church of God for the souls of men. Vastly larger, however, than any claim of ecclesiasticism is the sphere of the ministry which the present age suggests. Employers of labor promoting justice; artisans serving God with their hands; patient bearers of burdens and brave protestants against wrong; the thinkers of God's thoughts and the doers of God's will; nurses tending the poor and physicians risking their lives, — what are these, and many more whose social service has become personal joy, but ministers of a socialized religion and instruments of God's purpose for their own time? Never was the ministry of religion, thus defined, more compelling in its call; and never were its ranks more loyally filled. Never had preachers of religion and pastors of churches a better right to hopefulness than in this reënforcement of their own work with unanticipated allies. The ministry of religion associates in one vocation all who seek first God's Kingdom and His righteousness; and many a solitary servant of that cause takes heart again as he finds himself thus surrounded by a cloud of witnesses, and runs with greater patience the race which is set before him.

Here then, at last, the approach to the Social Question seems to reach its end. Up the dusty road of social science the traveler trudges until the walls of the city come into view. Over those walls he looks toward the spires of sociology. Up to the gate he comes, by the economic highway, and knocks at the porter's lodge; and the key of ethics opens the gate into the meaning of the modern world. Along the main thoroughfare of ethical idealism he marches toward the end of his search, and finds himself at last where all roads converge, as in a cathedral square; and entering the temple of religion he is led up the aisle of faith into the immediate presence of the living God. And here, in this quieting sense that the Social Question is God's way of persuasion to the mind of the present age, he finds rest from the noises of the time, as though the church door closed behind him and left him before the altar. The final justification of hope and courage among the perplexities and perturbations of the present age is in this final recognition of a religious significance in the Social Question. Imperfect, tentative, experimental, these social schemes and dreams may be, but they have their share in the large purpose of the Eternal. These troubled agitations, these vain experiments, these disappointing schemes, these repeated failures, all have their part in God's education of the human race. Our little systems have their day within the permanence and patience of God. Round our incompleteness flows His completeness; round our restlessness His rest. We began with social science; we end with social religion. We began with works; we end with faith. We began with our own plans of social redemption; we end by casting them all into the great movement of the Divine Will. "He maketh the devices of the people," it is written, "of none effect," but "the counsel of the Lord standeth for ever, the thoughts of his heart to all generations."[1]

[1] Ps. xxxiii. 10, 11.

INDEX OF NAMES AND SUBJECTS

Adler, Felix, 80.
Æsthetics, see Art; Beauty.
American Journal of Sociology, 47; 50 *note;* 67 *note.*
American Social Science Association, 28.
Americans, character of the, 6; 158-164.
Anarchism, 110.
Anselm, 183.
Aquinas, Thomas, on relation between ethics and political economy, 87-88.
Aristotle, 16, 89; social philosophy of, 12; on relation between ethics and political economy, 87.
Arnold, Matthew, 163.
Art, 3, 137-144.
Association Internationale pour le Progrès des Sciences Sociales, 28.
Atlantic Monthly, 66 *note.*
Augustine, 175.
Aveling, E., 61 *note;* 170 *note.*

Bacon, Francis, on relation of pure to applied science, 77-78; on uses of moral knowledge, 100.
Baldwin, J. M., 11.
Balfour, Arthur, on nature of sociology, 49-50.
Bastiat, on economic harmony, 55.
Beauty, 137-144.
Bebel, August, on woman, 38-39; on transformation to result from socialism, 62-63; on religion, 169-170.
Bentham, 136; doctrine of prudentialism, 119-120.
Bernstein, 68 *note.*

Booth, Charles, work of, 42-45.
Bridges, 46 *note.*
Brougham, *Lord,* 28.
Business, religion and, 193-195.
Butcher, S. H., 13.

Carlyle, denunciation of political economy, 69-74.
Chalmers, 64.
Channing, 200.
Charity, science and sentiment in, 91-93; in terms of egoism, prudentialism, and idealism, 150-153; and religion, 166-167, 192-193; idealism in charity work, 192-193.
Chase, 87 *note.*
Christianity, teaching of social interdependence, 13; original appeal to the individual, 15; religion and Social Question, Ch. VI.
Church, The, mission of, 198-199.
Cicero, 24; 25 *note.*
Commercialism, in U. S., 158-164.
Competition, see *Laissez faire.*
Comte, August, inventor of word "sociology," 14, 46; on nature of sociology, 46-49.
Cooley, C. H., 11.
Coöperation, origin of word, 14.
Correlation, in science and in Social Question, 33-40.
Courtney, W. L., 117, 133.

Dante, 125; 195.
Democracy, extension to industry, 3.
De Quincey, on work of Ricardo, 54-55.

INDEX OF NAMES AND SUBJECTS

Dickinson, Lowes, on American character, 6; type of socialism, 66-67.
Duty, *see* Egoism, Prudentialism, Idealism, Ethics.

Economic determinism, 61-65.
Economics, and the Social Question, Ch. III; a pure or an applied science, 53-54, 74-78; revolt of workingmen against, 59-60; and socialism, 60-69; protest of Carlyle and Ruskin against, 69-74; relation to social reform, 75-78; relation to ethics in labor struggles, 78-86; related to ethics as machinery to power, 86-95.
Egoism, exposition and criticism, 111-119; in the family, 147-150; in charity, 150-153; in industry, 153-158; in national life, 158-164.
Emotion, *see* Feeling.
Emerson, R. W., 125; 144.
Engels, 67; on Marx's fundamental proposition, 62-63; on religion, 169-170.
Erfurt Programme 1891, 168.
Ethics, individualistic, 9-10; its new social note, 10-16; Social Question a moral question, 78-90; as motive in labor struggles, 79-86; and economics, 86-95; and the Social Question, Ch. IV; as study of life in process, 96-100; essentially a social science, 101-103; individual freedom in social service, 107-110; egoism, prudentialism, and idealism as regulators of conduct, 111-135; of the family, charity, industry, and national life, 147-164.
Ezekiel, 92.

Family, The, correlation with other social problems, 34-36; socialism's attitude towards, 38-39; an economic or ethical fact, 93-94; interpreted in terms of egoism, prudentialism, and idealism, 147-150.
Feeling, as guide in religion, 176-188.
Feltham, Owen, on relation between contemplation and action, 22.
Ferri, on religion, 170.
Fichte, 139; on religion as service, 177-178.
Fiske, John, on correlation of forces, 40, 45; on relation between science and philosophy, 45; on relation between natural and ethical, 116.
Fox, George, 183.
Fremantle, 17.

Generalization, in science and in Social Question, 31-33.
George, Henry, on moral wrong as source of social evils, 79.
Giddings, on nature of sociology, 17, 48-49.
Goldsmith, 125.
Gompers, Samuel, on religion and workingmen, 168.
Greek philosophy, the State an organism, 11-12.
Green, T. H., moral idealism of, 132.
Grote, J., 133; 144.

Haldane, 88 *note;* on scientific abstraction, 77.
Halsted, 32 *note.*
Hamilton, *Sir* William, 25 *note.*
Harnack, 157.
Hartenstein, 22 *note;* 108 *note.*
Hayes-Robbins, 167.
Hegel, on function of philosophy, 25; on rationalism in religion, 177.
Hibbert Journal, 67 *note;* 68 *note.*

INDEX OF NAMES AND SUBJECTS

Hobbes, his doctrine of egoism, 112-114, 117, 118, 119, 136.
Holtzendorff, v., 87 *note*.
Holyoake, G. J., 14 *note*.
Housing, correlation with other social problems, 36-37, 151-152.
Howard, John, 200.
Howe, S. G., 200.
Huxley, on contrast between cosmic process and ethical process, 116.

Idealism, in modern socialism, 65-66; motive power of struggle of laboring class, 79-86; as regulator of moral conduct, 123-135; and the Social Question, Ch. V; in pursuit of truth, art, and goodness, 137-144; in the family, 147-150; in charity, 150-153, 192-193; in industry, 153-158; in national life, 158-164; in religion, 176-188.
Individual, The, problem of adjustment in family, philanthropy, and industry, 19.
Individualism, in modern philosophy, 9-10; in Greek philosophy, 11-13; in modern jurisprudence, legislation, ethics, and religion, 16-19; in religion, 196-197.
Industry, *see* Labor Question.
Isaiah, 175.

Jacks, L. P., on Church and World, 167.
James, on the selves within the self, 118.
Jesus, 25, 130, 144, 166; social ideal of, 13-14; on the worth of the individual, 15-16; his self-dedication to human service, 173-176, 198, 200; his appeal to the will, 185-188; both ethical teacher and religious leader, 186-188.
Jevons, 57.

Jodl, F., 87 *note*.
Jones, Henry, 164 *note*.
Jones, Rufus, 180 *note*.
Journal of Social Science, 28.
Jowett, Benjamin, 12 *note;* 24 *note;* 132 *note;* 143 *note;* on influence of ideals, 144.
Jurisprudence, new note of, 16.

Kant, 136; 145; 177; on relation between observation and reflection, 22; on freedom in service, 108; moral idealism of, 132.
Kaufmann, M., 171 *note*.
Kepler, 142.
Keynes, J. N., 54 *note;* 55 *note;* 56, 75.
Klein, F., 30.
Knowledge, dependent on both observation and reflection, 21-22.

Labor Question, ethical nature of, 79-86, 94-95; in terms of egoism, prudentialism, and idealism, 153-158; and religion, 167-168.
Laissez faire, in theory and practice, 53-61; connection with origin of socialism, 60-65; treatment at hands of Carlyle and Ruskin, 69-74.
La Monte, R. R., 170 *note*.
La Réforme Sociale, 42 *note*.
Lang, Andrew, 87 *note*.
Laplace, 170.
Lassalle, on the iron law of wages, 60.
Launfal, *Sir*, 193.
Le Play, Frédéric, life and work of, 41-43, 45.
Lewes, on character and circumstances, 64.
Lexis, on justice in industry, 157.
Liebknecht, on religion, 171.
Liquor problem, The, correlation with other social problems, 37.
Locke, 117.
London Spectator, 127; 166.

London Times, 63 *note.*
Longfellow, 126 *note.*
Lotze, on moral purpose in universe, 89–90.
Lowell, 12 *note;* 141; on relation of theory to practice, 21.

Maine, *Sir* Henry S., 15.
Malthus, 56.
Martineau, Harriet, 47 *note;* 48 *note.*
Martineau, on religion as service, 177–178.
Marx, on his connection with orthodox economics, 60–61; his materialism and economic determinism, 61–68; on religion, 168–170.
Mazaryk, 68 *note.*
Mazzini, on individual and society, 18.
Melbourne, *Lord*, 187.
Mencken, 114 *note.*
Metaphysics, place in social interpretations, 44–46.
Mill, John Stuart, 75; summary of Bentham's view of prudentialism, 120.
Ministry, The, and social service, 199–202.
Molesworth, 112 *note.*
Motley, 192.
Muirhead, definition of philosophy, 25.
Mysticism, in religion, 176–188.

National Association for the Promotion of Social Science, 28.
National life, in terms of egoism, prudentialism, and idealism, 158–164.
Newton, 109.
Nietzsche, his doctrine of egoism, 74, 113–119, 122, 129–130, 136, 154.

Observation, relation to reflection, 20–23; place in scientific method, 28–29; application to Social Question, 29–31.
Oliphant, Laurence, 195.
Ostwald, on morality a social phenomenon, 101–102.
Owen, Robert, originated word "coöperation," 14.

Paine, Robert Treat, 91.
Paley, 183.
Palmer, on ethics and life, 99.
Paul, 132; social teaching, 13, 18; on unity of mankind, 198–199.
Paulsen, on reason and will, 178.
Peabody, F. G., 33 *note;* 35 *note;* 179 *note.*
Pearson, Karl, on socialism and the family, 38.
Perry, 143 *note;* on philosophical thinking, 25; on morality as an economy or community of interests, 103; criticism of egoism, 117.
Personality, a discovery of Jesus, 15; the centre of economic, moral, and religious concern, 16.
Philanthropy, Sumner's criticism of, 56–58; science and sentiment in, 91–93.
Philosophy, and the Social Question, Ch. I; and other knowledge, 20–24; as the unification of knowledge, 24–25.
Physiological psychology, 23.
Pitt, William, *Sir*, 88.
Plato, on individual and State, 11–12; on philosophy and wisdom, 24; moral idealism of, 132, 136, 145; on beauty and goodness, 143.
Poincaré, H. 32.
Polenz, von, on American character, 159.
Politics, *see* National Life.
Poverty, relation to misfortune and misconduct, 36.
Protestantism, 15.

Proudhon, condemnation of political economy, 59.
Prudentialism, exposition and criticism of, 119–130; in the family, 147–150; in charity, 150–153; in industry, 153–158; in national life, 158–164.
Pythagoras, definition of a philosopher, 24–25.

Rabbeth, Dr. Samuel, 127.
Rationalism, in religion, 176–188.
Reason, as guide in religion, 176–188.
Reflection, relation to observation, 20–23.
Reform, dangers of precipitate, 4–7; relation of theory to action, 7–8.
Regulus, 126, 131.
Religion, its present concern, the world, 15–17; and the Social Question, Ch. VI; and charity, 165–167, 192–193; and laborers, 167–168; and socialism, 168–171; rationalism, mysticism, and idealism in, 176–188; and business, 193–195; and individualism, 195–197; and social service, 198–202.
Ricardo, 56; 60; 61; on harmony between self-interest and the common good, 54–55.
Robertson, Frederic, 178.
Robinson Crusoe, 9–10.
Romilly, Samuel, *Sir*, 89 *note*.
Royce, Josiah, on organization of experience, 32; on the moral law, 104.
Ruskin, proposed reformation of political economy, 69–74, 78.

Sabatier, 179.
Schleiermacher, mysticism of, 177.
Schmoller, Gustav, on social nature of man, 10; on nature of sociology, 49; on industrial life both a natural and ethical system, 79; on American character, 159.
Science, its method, and application to Social Question, 28–44; its work preliminary, 40–41; its relation to metaphysics, 44; "pure" and "applied," 53–54, 74–78.
Scudder, Vida D., 67 *note*.
Senior, N. W., 54.
Small, A. W., 48; 50.
Small and Vincent, on nature of sociology, 48.
Smith, 177 *note*.
Smith, Adam, 61; 77; on harmony between self-interest and the common good, 54–55; on relation of ethics to political economy, 87–89.
Social Museum, as instrument of instruction, 30–33.
Social organism, 14, 17.
Social Science, and the Social Question, 28–45.
Socialism, attitude towards the family, 38; relation to doctrine of *laissez faire*, 60–65; materialism and economic determinism of founders, 62–68; moral idealism of some present-day exponents, 66–67; and religion, 168–171.
Society, difficulties of present, 1–7; organic, 8–11, 17–18; and individual, 15–17; biological form or psychological process, 17–18; philosophy of, 25–26; correlation of social questions, 33–40.
Sociology, and Comte, 14; and Social Question, 45–52; relation to other sciences, 47–50.
Soldiers Field, Harvard University, 124.
Spargo, John, type of socialism, 67.
Spedding, 100 *note*.
Spencer, Herbert, 49; 136; on social organism, 14, 17; on

INDEX OF NAMES AND SUBJECTS

conservation and transformation of energy, 34; on the Unknowable — the Infinite and Eternal Energy, 44–45; as teacher of prudentialism, 120–124; on sense of obligation, 132–133.

State, The, Greek conception of, 11–13.

Stein, on social reconstruction the task of present century, 1; on science and moral obligation, 47; on Social Question a moral question, 59, 83; on materialism as the basis of Marx's system, 65; on isolated individual an abstraction, 103.

Stevenson, Robert Louis, 25.
Stirling, 55 *note*.
Stone, 62 *note*.
Sumner, W. G., on what social classes owe each other, 56–58; on economics as a "pure" science, 58.

Tennyson, 121.
Theory, need of, 7–8.
Thilly, Frank, 178 *note*.

Toynbee, Arnold, 60; on free competition, 56.
Truth, 24, 137–139.
Tyndall, 142.

United States, commercialism in, 158–164.

Villard, H., 28 *note*.
Virgil, 126.

Wage-earners, motive of moral idealism in class struggles, 79–86.
Wagner, A., 54.
Wallace, 25 *note;* morality only in society, 102.
Ward, L. F., on nature of sociology, 48.
Warner, A. G., 36 *note*.
Welfare work, attitude of wage-earners towards, 84–86.
Wesley, John, 200.
Whitefield, 183.
Will, in religion, 176–188.
Winstanley, 180.

Ziegler, Th., 5 *note;* 87 *note*.

www.ingramcontent.com/pod-product-compliance
Lightning Source LLC
Chambersburg PA
CBHW071439150426
43191CB00008B/1179